Faith Comes By Hearing

Paul Doty

Edited by Shawn Gray

Faith Comes By Hearing edition v1.9

Copyright 2018
(c)P & L Authors

Dedication

When I set out to write this book, I knew full well that it would not be a New York Best Seller due to its niche audience, therefore it is dedicated to you, the reader, and all those who have sat through any of my classes in the past. All those who would desire to better their own understanding of sound and sound science in order to further the kingdom of God.

About the Author

The first time I met Paul was when he did sound for my band at the State Theater in Modesto, California, back in 1996.

He was the best soundman I had ever heard. And he had the worst haircut I'd ever seen.

He's still the best soundman I've ever worked with, and his choice of hairstyle has improved immensely over time.

We've been working together for the past 20 years, and there are many things that continue to impress me. He pays attention to detail. He shows up early and stays late. He keeps improving his skills, stays updated on all the latest gear and technology, and does all this with verve, humility, and humor.

But the thing that impressed me most was when I told him I wanted to do a live Slim Man album a few years ago. He sent me about 20 CDs (remember them?) of shows that he had recorded over the past two decades. I had no idea that Paul had recorded so many of my concerts. I listened to them while taking a road trip from Nashville to Baltimore, Maryland, my hometown.

The sound that came out of the car stereo was stellar, stunning, clear, and amazing. Paul had studied the music so thoroughly that he knew when every sax solo was coming up, he knew where every percussion breakdown was, he had all his effects—reverbs, delays—set to the tempo of each song. The balance between instruments and vocals was near-perfect. It was truly impressive.

But the thing that was most mind-blowing?

I was listening to a two-track live mix. In other words, Paul didn't record each track individually, go to a studio, and mix each song. What I was hearing was exactly what the audience had heard straight off his mixing console. He mixed each song on the spot and on the fly. What I was listening to in my car on that road trip was a magnificent and glorious soundscape of a master engineer who had captured performances with balance and precision.

And he made it all sound so effortless and wonderful. The only problem with the Slim Man Live CD is that I had too many excellent-sounding songs to choose from!

I don't throw the "G" word around a lot, but Paul is a genius at what he does. He truly cares, he's got very high standards, and he delivers way beyond expectations.

And he's a great guy to hang out with.

Cheers!

Recording artist & author,
Slim Man

Sound Doctrine	1
Sound Credentials	9
Sound Explained	19
Sound Science	29
The Medium	37
Rings, Feedback, and Other Things That Drive You Nuts	46
Garbage In, Garbage Out	55
Sound System Fundamentals	62
Biology & Acoustics	74
Reverberation	81
If Bad Sound Were Toxic, We'd All Be Dead	88
Mic Choice	106
Mic Technique	114
Tonality	128
Getting the Mix	138
Effects	147
Monitor World	156
Engineering Secrets Revealed	164
Light Of The World	173
The Art Of Troubleshooting	184
Isn't That Special	193
Psycho Acoustics	200

Chapter 1

Sound Doctrine

They say that those who can, do, and those who can't, teach. I have been doing *and* teaching sound reinforcement and production for forty years. As I begin this book, my career in sound is likely drawing to a close; as I approach my sixties, retirement to some degree lies just around the corner. Retirement will bring closure to one of the longest chapters of my life, at least the *doing* part. With the advent of this book, it's my hope that the teaching part might go on for some time, possibly even outliving me.

When I set out to write this book, I could have easily simply written a technical manual for any and all engineers out there doing sound in any venue, from a nightclub to a concert arena, but as a born-again Christian, I have chosen to focus on sound for the house of worship. If you are reading this book and are not a Christian, you will still gain valuable knowledge to the technical side of the art of sound reinforcement, but know that this book will also reflect its authors beliefs and personal faith. For me, it's hard to separate the two nor do I feel compelled to do so.

Although this book is geared primarily for church sound engineers, it will also be quite suited for anyone on the opposite end of the console as well. If you are a pastor, worship leader, worship team member, recording artist, or anyone who has an opportunity to interact with sound people, it's always beneficial to have a strong understanding of what your engineer deals with every time they sit down at the console. All too often, the artists on the mic end of the chain find themselves at odds with the person on the console end. No good can come of this as both ends are on the same team. The more that both ends of the chain become a well oiled and coordinated machine, the more efficient and effective the result will be and the more pleasant the experience will be for everyone involved.

Before I begin I would like to take a moment to thank all of the pastors that have encouraged me to write this book. Their enthusiasm for this project has only further underscored for me the need for a book such as this to exist.

Faith Comes by Hearing
I had a pastor once who instilled in me the fact that every time we walk into a sanctuary to share the realities of God, His nature, and His saving grace with people, there is life and death in the room. As the church sound engineer, we are charged with overseeing the ability for the people in our church to truly hear without the sound being a distraction. Romans 10:17 states that *faith comes by hearing*. We need to understand the soberness of the part of the service for which we are responsible. We can balance this perspective with the notion that sound is fun. We have the privilege of serving God and others through an art that can be considered a gift from Him.

I am seldom the guy in the pews of a church with my hands raised in worship. I was designed by my creator to worship with my technical talents. I can look out over a congregation on a Sunday morning with its hands raised and enjoy the corporate worship with everyone, but I'm most worshipful when my hands are on faders.

* * *

Romans 12:1-8 states, I appeal to you therefore, brothers, by the mercies of God, to present your bodies as a living sacrifice, holy and acceptable to God, which is your spiritual worship. Do not be conformed to this world, but be transformed by the renewal of your mind, that by testing you may discern what is the will of God, what is good and acceptable and perfect. For by the grace given to me I say to everyone among you not to think of himself more highly than he ought to think, but to think with sober judgment, each according to the measure of faith that God has assigned. For as in one body we have many members, and the members do not all have the same function, so we, though many, are one body in Christ, and individually members one of another. Having gifts that differ according to the grace given to us, let us use them: if prophecy, in proportion to our faith; if service, in our serving; the one who teaches, in his teaching; the one who exhorts, in his exhortation; the one who contributes, in generosity; the one who leads, with zeal; the one who does acts of mercy, with cheerfulness.

Sound is Balance

As with everything in life, it is the same with sound, there is a need for balance. The sound ministry is like a teeter-totter. On one side we must understand the weight of that life and death/eternity scenario every time we power up the system. On any given Sunday, quality sound with minimal distraction is mission critical.

On the other hand, this must be balanced with the fact that *you're not as important as you think you are*. That is to say, God will use anything and anybody to make sure His word goes forth. While we don't want to sell short the importance of what we do, we never want to enter into a place of arrogance about it either. Your place in the ministry team is a gift from Him, a privilege. The sound ministry is not about you. It is about Him, and it's about service. Becoming self-focussed is a sure way to limit the effectiveness of your ministry.

While fun, the sound ministry is filled with challenges. There are intellectual challenges in learning the equipment and techniques for using it. There are the artistic challenges to push beyond the robotic into the realm of artistic engagement with your listener. There are the physical challenges of fatigue on your body. Then there are the spiritual challenges that you often times don't see coming until they blindside you, as you step out into an endeavor that will have direct results in furthering the kingdom of God.

Anytime we enter into a support role in the Body of Christ, we essentially paint a bullseye on our back. Attacks can come into a service from a multitude of angles. It's not always the massive equipment failure. More often than not, it can be as simple as the small distractions that creep in when things are just a little bit wrong, just a little bit ringy, just a little bit tinny, or anything really, that causes a distraction.

A chain will only be as strong as its weakest link, and you are the final human link on the pastor's, *faith comes by hearing* chain. If you've never had experience with what people refer to as spiritual warfare, welcome to the sound ministry! It will be there and it will be unavoidable. Trust me, you will become well acquainted with it in a relatively short amount of time.

Time, Rust, Laundry, and Technology Never Sleep

If you are going to be involved in sound, lighting, or virtually any area of technology today whether it be computers, web programming, etc., you are going to be involved in an area in which you will never stop learning. On the day you begin to feel that you have learned it all, or that you know it all, you will be able to put a stopwatch on your craft as to how much longer you will last doing it. Your effectiveness will fall by the wayside, because with all technology today, it is growing at a pace that literally no single human being on the planet can keep up with. The great sound engineer is not the one who knows it all. It's the one who knows *what he doesn't know*. It's the one that never stops learning and applying. It's the one who can observe others without jealousies and apply the lessons he or she learns from them.

We live in an unprecedented time in world history of technological growth. At the same time, we live in a time of unprecedented attack on the morals and foundation of Christianity. I believe these two truths are directly related. We've never had a time in human history that technology has played such a widespread role in reaching the planet for Christ. At the same time, the opposition to that outreach has increased proportionally. Consequently, it's an extremely exciting time to be involved in service through technology.

Control Freaks

As for those who are drawn to sound, I have a great appreciation and respect for those who have embraced this calling on their lives. While I love our worship team members and pastors and have great respect for them as well, you seldom have to wonder about the motivation of a sound engineer. The soundman's position is one of service. We seldom have the exposure and accolades of someone on stage, and the audience seldom pays any attention to us whatsoever, until perhaps, something goes wrong, or something's not heard, or something's too loud.

Our personalities have been designed to be control freaks, and that fits our task at hand like a piece in a jigsaw puzzle. What could be a bad trait in another individual, is perfectly useful in us as we balance and temper that trait with control. We are wired a bit differently here in the sound ministry. Embrace that. I have always marveled at how many individuals in the body of Christ seem to be called to be a worship musician, and how few seem to be called to be a soundman.

Rubber Meets the Road
The Bible tells us not to forsake the assembly of the brethren. In fact, if you do a simple word search in your Bible, you'll be amazed at how many times the word assembly is used where you or I might have chosen the word gather. In fact, it can be seen this way throughout scripture, not in just one or two books, but throughout. It's as if the Holy Spirit is conveying a thought through the entirety of Scripture to us when it comes to the Body of Christ. For those who have read my first book Rubber Meets the Road, you'll note that I talked about this there, and I still feel that it's important enough to note it again here.

We were never meant to simply gather together as a collection. It has always been God's intention that we assemble ourselves together like one does when they build or assemble a table from Ikea. The thought is that we are all unique parts, purpose-built to meet the different needs of the body.

Now if you're a worship person reading this book, or any other non-sound person, please know that I'm not questioning your choice or calling. Nor am I suggesting that you should become a sound engineer. The very fact that you're reading this book demonstrates to me that you are a person who wants to understand how this whole team fits together cohesively for the furthering of God's kingdom. I'm just letting you in on my perspective of what I've been able to observe as someone who has spent many years working with churches.

Good Help Is Hard To Find

Any pastor knows how hard it is to find good service people when it comes to sound. We've all heard weekly pleadings from the pulpit for help with the sound team. It seems there is always a need for people to get involved in sound ministry.

When I go to a church for the first time as an advisor, I will observe all of the issues surrounding the sound system in that church. You look for the weak links and start improving what the church needs the most. You consider the acoustics of the room. You consider the quality of the worship team. You look at the quality and functionality of the gear, and you consider the technicians running it. In almost every situation, the church's main focus of improvement will be on the gear, while the weakest link, more often than not, lies in one or more of the other three.

I'll also mention in passing, if you're a woman reading this book, thank you, and praise God for you! Even in the professional sound industry, women who are willing to enter this field are still far and few between. And why should that be? The sound ministry knows no gender bounds. I'll go on the record saying that the majority of the female engineers that I have had the pleasure of working with over the years I would place in the *excellent* category. Perhaps this is due to the fact that they have had to compete in a male-dominated segment of music production, but for whatever reason, most of the women who go into this area, seem to do extremely well. So let's go gals! Bring it on! Represent!

We use the term soundman for both male and female in the generic man-kind way, and know that every time I use it in this book, ladies you are included. I look forward to a time in the future when we can add common all-encompassing phraseology to our sound vocabulary. Where terms like *sound person* might become as natural and all-encompassing as a term like *snowboarder*, or *gamer*.

Let's Get Going!

In closing this introductory chapter, I trust everyone is ready to dig in. While we've touched on the challenges of doing this job, running sound is still fun. It will create a camaraderie between you and the people around you and it will give you a solid place to serve in the Body of Christ. It will provide a place for your growth mentally, physically, and spiritually. It will teach others to trust in you, and it will teach you to trust in others. It's a place of learning truths about your creator in ways you might not be able to otherwise. It is a blessed place of creativity, where creative people can fit into the jigsaw puzzle of life. As you embrace the place that God has designed you for, enjoy the journey of learning and discovery. It will never stop.

Chapter 2

Sound Credentials

First Things First

This book will not be autobiographical in nature, but before we delve into the instruction, tips, and tricks of the forthcoming chapters, I want to take the first few chapters for you to get to know me better. As such this chapter will serve as a mini-biography to fill you in on my credentials, experience, and philosophies.

Growing up as a kid I was a bit of a geek. You remember, in school there were always nerds and geeks. The nerds were on the nerdy awkward side and the geeks were on the nerdy obsessed technical side. As it turns out, fortunately for me, the nerds and the geeks ended up growing up to run the world.

Okay, perhaps that's a nerdy exaggeration, but then again if you look at the Bill Gates, Steve Jobs, Elon Musk, and the Amazon computer-based internet economy and technology of the world today, perhaps not. I'm willing to bet that a lot of you reading this book didn't quite fit in while growing up. Many of those traits that set you apart, many of those curiosities, many of those interests just may serve you well now in the field of sound. You too may indeed find out that God has been preparing you for something a bit different all the while.

Physical & Spiritual

This book comes at the task of teaching sound from the unique angle of both the physical and the spiritual. I was raised in a Christian home, and I see the world through the eyes of a Christian. I came to know Christ at a very early age. In a real sense, I can honestly say that I do not know what it is like to not be a Christian.

* * *

In my near sixty years, I have attended four different churches, the last three being non-denominational/evangelical. If I had to give myself a religious label, I would describe myself as an intelligent design creationist. I know that's more of a description than a title, but it's simply to say that I see the world, in all of its design, and I enjoy and commune with my creator through it.

A Brief Statement of Faith
I am a literal creationist who believes that God created the world exactly as recorded in Genesis, over a literal seven day period and that He spoke everything into existence that is. I believe that He is responsible for all the rules in science that govern our very existence. I believe that mankind is the purpose for that creation and was uniquely created for the purpose of worship, fellowship, and friendship with Him. I believe that our uniqueness can be seen from the very beginning, considering that God took a completely different turn in the creation process by actually forming us with His very hands as opposed to simply speaking us into existence like everything else.

My relationship with Jesus starts with the acknowledgment and the wonderment of John 1:1 that states that **In the beginning was the Word, and the Word was with God, and the Word was God. He was in the beginning with God. All things were made through him, and without him was not anything made that was made.**

It ends with the hope and trust of an eternity with Him, an everlasting continuation of the relationship we've begun here in the physical, and I know that it was only possible through *His* part of restoring our relationship through His death on a cross some 2000 years ago, **for God so loved the world, that he gave his only Son, that whoever believes in him should not perish but have eternal life. For God did not send his Son into the world to condemn the world, but in order that the world might be saved through him. Whoever believes in him is not condemned, but whoever does not believe is condemned already, because he has not believed in the name of the only Son of God.**

* * *

My enjoyment and fulfillment in this life lie between those two bookends as I'm able to worship and enjoy him with the talents He has given me. This should be the foundation of everything we do as children of God. It is a God-given need in our hearts to share Him with a lost world, and it should serve as our motivation and purpose in the sound ministry.

I suppose every profession see's God through its own eye's, but I feel particularly blessed to have lived the near entirety of my life involved in sound. Through the study of sound you will find a unique glimpse into God's creation and if your eyes are open, you will see His design in ways a non-engineer will miss. From the invisible world of sound & acoustics to the complex design of the human brain and auditory system, you will begin to see the plan, code, and execution of an incomparably superior programmer and engineer.

Early Years

I began my career in sound and lighting in my late teens, at the end of the seventies and the start of the eighties. I cut my teeth behind sound consoles during the hair metal band era of the eighties with two of the biggest groups in Christian rock music, Barren Cross and Christian Music Hall of Fame members Bloodgood. I'm still friends with both bands to this day, and on rare occasions when either step out of retirement for an appearance, it's not uncommon to find me behind one of their consoles.

* * *

L-R: Michael Bloodgood, Paul Doty, Les Carlsen

When I began, there was no digital audio, and computer technology was in its infancy. Racks and racks of outboard gear were the norm. In those day's you often had to manufacture your own specialized pieces of equipment, as products were not plentiful like today.

Electronics was my road into the sound reinforcement industry. I majored in electronics and electronic mathematics in high school and began building audio gear in my late teens. I liked music and likely would have learned to play guitar or bass if it weren't for an injury I received to a finger on my left hand at an early age.

When I was four or five, my oldest sister accidentally caught my middle finger in a car door. I lost the end of it just above the last joint. Some of it was able to be reattached, but unfortunately, the tip was not salvageable, and this left me with exposed nerve endings on it. Later in life, pressing down on guitar strings turned out to be an irritating reminder of what had happened so many years before. So,

I entered the world of music through electronics, and where technology, electronics, and music came together was in sound reinforcement.

In a true sense, I really have my sister to thank for my career direction. As I approach 60, I can look back at my life through the lens of hindsight. I have learned to appreciate the many twists and turns that weave through our lives, the things that we may at first see as random tragedies that later develop into a tapestry of life woven together by our Creator for our good.

A Life of Experience
Throughout this book, I will be sharing the practical science, knowledge, and experience I have accumulated over the forty years of my career, but it will be laced with the personality and perspective of an engineer, saved by grace. I want the reader to be equally immersed in not only the technical side of our craft but in the worship aspect of it as well.

The sixties and seventies were an amazing time in music history for a kid to grow up. When I look back at the state of the art in sound reinforcement in 1978 and compare it with that of 2018, it underscores the fact that both technology, and I, have lived an entire life of change and refinement.

Change
It's amazing to look back over forty years and see the things that have changed and the things that have stayed the same. Consoles and the way we process sound have probably changed the most in the last forty years, but the physics of sound and the laws that govern it never will, so while this book may need to be updated every few years as the gear in the industry changes, the physics of sound and the principles of what we do as engineers will not.

For example, amplifiers have become considerably lighter over the years and the internal components have improved, but the basics of what an amplifier does through electronics has stayed pretty much the same. Loudspeaker technology has moved past the traditional point and shoot square box, to the array-able trapezoid cabinet, and then on to the acoustically superior line array design, but the principles and the mathematics of sound and methods of reproduction have not changed.

Essentially, it's a hundred years into sound reproduction, and we're still using paper to push air. What all of this means for the reader is that while the gear references in this book will surely become quaint and antiquated someday in the near future, the principals of engineering and the physics of sound itself will never change.

I started in sound as a soundman for local bands and as a soundman for a young church upstart in my hometown. I was in high school and I was armed only with the desire to do it. In the beginning, I lacked any formal training other than an electronics background and a love for music. My initial attempts to do sound were an ongoing exercise in trial and lots of error. In the early days, I had no real mentor to speak of, and I would learn a piece of gear simply by attempting to use it. I would use the P.U.S.H. method of learning (Push Until Something Happens). My efforts in the first few years were met with predictably limited results, but what I learned the most, was that I really enjoyed it, and I wanted to learn more. What I didn't fully realize was that the learning process that I was embarking upon, was going to last a lifetime.

As I look back on my career it's interesting for me to note that throughout my life, I have always seemed to return to my roots as a church sound engineer in some form or capacity, whether by doing, teaching, or overseeing. This book is even a continuation of that path.

After high school, I began designing and building my own pieces of musical electronic gear, compressors, limiters and the like. I would offer many of my pieces up for sale in the newspaper, and that eventually caught the eye of a semi-local production company owner who eventually hired me to be his system designer and bench tech.

Education

My formal training came in the form of the Recording Institute of America. Full Sail would become a popular school for budding sound engineers in the 80s, but in the mid to late 70s, the school of choice for certification in sound engineering was RIA. I graduated RIA in the late 70s with a certification in multitrack recording and sound science.

I'm often asked what importance a college or trade school plays in a career in audio. My answer as both a graduate *and* a business owner is that while all education is extremely important, nothing compares with seat time and aptitude. Whether in the position of an employer or an overseer of the sound ministry at a church, I am always looking at aptitude and experience over formal education. I have had people fresh out of college or Full Sail apply for employment at my company, but I'll give the guy a shot who's already had a year going to the school of hard knocks out in the real world. The bottom line is that education is great, whether from a formal school, the internet, an instructor like myself, a book, or a class; but there are no shortcuts when it comes to seat time and real-world experience, pressure, and problem-solving.

Now if you've just started your journey in sound, and you do not as yet have a history of experience, don't feel discouraged! Like playing any musical instrument, anyone can jump into sound at any level and begin getting raw sound out of a sound system! As we start our journey, God is not so much looking for *ability* as He is *availability*. If there is an aptitude and a desire to learn, all you need is the seat time. The experience will come.

Villa

After my formal education, I went to work at a legendary recording studio in Northern California called Villa Recorders. Villa was known back in its hay day as a world-class project studio and a frequent haunt of artists like Toto, Peter Frampton, Humble Pie, Edgar Winter, and Chicago. It was a stealthy little getaway studio located in the middle of an unassuming country orchard, about an hour and a half's drive from the San Francisco Bay area. Villa provided an opportunity to hone the skills I had learned at RIA in a real-world situation. Even though I would soon go exclusively into live sound reinforcement, my time there was foundational.

After Villa, I would soon transition into a full-time live sound engineer, and I would soon be seeking opportunities to minister with the gifts and talents I had been using at the studio.

Webster defines ministry as *a person or thing through which something is accomplished*. Service is defined as a *contribution to the welfare of others. Useful labor that does not produce a tangible commodity*.

The idea and adrenaline rush of flying by the seat of my pants, and working without a net, was appealing to me when I first started dabbling in live shows. These were the things that drew me from studio engineering into live sound. Yes, we may have a tangible product for lack of a better word when we post a sermon on a podcast, but for the most part, live sound in general and the sound ministry specifically is not a tangible service that produces a product. I think that rush had a lot to do with my eventual retirement as a studio engineer and my movement into being a full-time live sound engineer.

WCSL
In 1986 my wife and I founded West Coast Sound & Light, a Northern California based production company. Soon after WCSL was born, we would partner with another couple whom we had worked with in a band for five years prior. To say that we were committed to making a production company work would be an understatement. We actually took both of our budding families and moved them into the same house together for a number of years, just to be able to share the expenses needed in order to get the company off the ground.

*　*　*

When it comes to doing sound, either as a career or as a servant in a church, I do not believe in luck or chance. Throughout my career, I have always made a conscious effort to put myself in positions to learn and advance. This is the work and the commitment of learning sound as a craft.

WCSL in Oracle Arena

The Cadillac Club
In the 90s I landed a position with California Concerts. At the time it was California's second-largest concert company. I ended up as the production manager for The Cadillac Club in Fresno California. During that time I oversaw up to seven national acts a week coming through this well-known club. I provided production and/or ran the sound for some of the largest national acts touring the club circuits at that time. I learned the skills of venue management and gained the experience of running a crew.

My career has expanded my roles and experience to include live sound engineering, studio engineering, podcasting, production management, lighting design, intelligent light programming, video, instruction, and tour management. I have sat behind consoles for classic legendary entertainers like Bob Hope, Don Rickles, and Bob Eubanks. I've run the show for top classic rock artists, national country artists, and a who's who of politics. God has given me the opportunities to look down at my faders and realize that there are multiple Grammys on the other end. And possibly, most importantly, He has given me the opportunity to share and instill that knowledge and those talents of the craft in others for the furthering of His kingdom.

Chapter 3

Sound Explained

Now that you've survived the first few preliminary chapters of the book it's time to get down to business. The next few chapters will be textbook in nature so don't be discouraged or surprised if you don't retain 100% of the information packed into them. In fact, they tell us that when we are initially exposed to a new subject, our brain will only retain about 5% of what it hears or reads. The good news for you is that this is a book rather than a stuffy lecture in a college. You can always go back later and re-read these chapters.

Some of these concepts will not make any sense to you until you can apply them in the real world, so just take in what you can, be relaxed, and settle in with a good cup of coffee in a quiet place. If a paragraph flies over your head, don't worry about it. You just might be surprised at how much more these chapters make sense after doing sound for a year or so. For now, take in as much as you can and life experience will fill in the gaps.

This book will endeavor to take the reader beyond a place of simple cause and reaction. When people begin to do sound, their common method of operation is to mess with something to get a result. While exploration is not a bad thing in and of itself, I firmly believe that you will never become a good engineer until you understand the fundamentals of what you're trying to accomplish.

Don't Touch That!
It's a common occurrence for me to walk into a new church sound booth for the first time and see faders and knobs marked with tape, and messages like "Don't touch this" or "Don't move anything!" The truth of the matter is that all of those knobs on your console *do* move, and do so for a reason. If a person is attempting to

run sound by simply seeking a result to an action, they will never move past a place of *cause and reaction*. They will always be a slave to result and frustrated by *lack* of it. They will find themselves in a never-ending cycle of survival, never moving beyond, into a place of creativity and art.

In my mind, I have always had a distinction between the terms *Soundman* and *Sound Engineer*. A soundman is quite mechanical. He or she has mastered the basics of what they need to do, but they've never pushed successfully beyond that. The engineer, by contrast, has moved beyond the basics into the realm of understanding, design, and creativity. In a true sense, sound for them has become an art.

Contrary to popular belief, working professionally in the sound industry on any level is not the measure of whether a person has graduated from the level of *soundman*, into the level of *sound engineer*. As a business owner, I see all too many individuals floundering at sound in arenas with national acts. We've all been at a supposed professional event, only to leave that event with ears that hurt from a soundman who hasn't got a clue as too when a system or room has reached its saturation point.

Fortunately, on the flip side, I've also seen great engineers who have a deep understanding of their craft. In defining the two, the soundman simply dabbles in and around sound. By definition the engineer, engineers sound. He pictures it, plans it, and shapes it. He understands his equipment on a deeper level than simple acquaintance.

For instance, it's far more important to know the *whys* of a piece of gear than the *hows*. I have had sound people ask questions like, "How do I hook up this piece of gear into my system?" What the soundman actually needs to know is *why* do we need the piece, *what* is its relationship to the system as a whole, and then we can understand the choices of *where* it can patch in and *how* it can be effective. In the end, if you understand the why, you will understand the how.

During the book, I will continually refer to sound reinforcement from a professional standpoint. I fully realize that most individuals who are reading this book, are doing so to improve their ability as a soundman and have little to no intention to pursue sound as a career. That's okay. The more you are exposed to sound in a professional way, the better you will become at your craft on whatever level you choose to pursue it, from part-time hobbyist to full-blown touring engineer, to everything in between.

It's my intention to start you with the cart behind the horse. To get to this place, we must go back to the basics of what we are doing in order to lay a solid foundation on which to build our house. This chapter and those to come will take a basic look at the building blocks that are in play when we talk about sound and controlling it. The next few chapters will be the hardest chapters of the book to wrap your head around, but once you do, it will lay the foundation to understand all the chapters that follow.

A Fallen World
As Christians, we realize that this place is not our home. It can be likened unto a simulation of sorts. Think of it as a computer program running on a huge mainframe somewhere beyond our comprehension. In many ways, that's what it is. Mind you, my example is quite rudimentary, but its point is that we are operating in a created environment, with a set of rules and parameters that govern that program.

Sound, as with all things in life, has a set list of rules and laws that govern its program. The more we understand that program, and understand those rules, the more successful we will be in its environment. But it's not enough to simply understand laws and rules, we must go to the next level and align our actions within the guidelines of those rules and laws. The more that you are able to do this as an engineer, the more successful you will be. With sound, as with anything else in life, the more you fight against those laws and rules, the more dismal your efforts will become.

As we begin to learn the rules and laws of this game, we will run into a stubborn reality, a concept that will haunt us as engineers every time we sit down to practice our craft. Every time we do, whether we think about it consciously or not, we will be taken back to a very early place in time. As a sound engineer, you will always be reminded that we live in a fallen world.

As sound engineers, some traits that we all share by varying degrees is that we're control freaks and perfectionists. By definition, we control things. As we try our best to stay within the laws and rules of the game, it will not take you long to realize that the game is broken. We will struggle for perfection, but we'll never reach it. We will eventually find that sound is about compromise rather than perfection.

In this chapter, we are going to address the laws and rules that affect what we do as sound engineers. I fully believe that if anyone is going to go about the business of manipulating sound, it is absolutely foundational that that person has, at minimum, a rudimentary understanding of what sound actually is. This includes a basic understanding of musical mathematics, acoustics, and the biology of sound perception.

At this point, the reader may be recoiling a bit while thinking, "All I want to do is be a good church soundman. I'm not looking for a degree here." Never fear, I hope to present this information in such a way that the weekend warrior will easily digest, but at the same time, I will do you a disservice if I offer you a grade school dumbing down of the physics involved. You may not track with everything we're going to pore over in this chapter and those to come, but you'll likely come away with a good overview and understanding of the fundamentals, at the very least, those fundamentals necessary for an educated background in what you are doing behind the console.

* * *

What is sound?
I know everyone will want to jump right into the tricks that make an engineer a wizard behind the console, but before we begin turning the knobs of technique, we must first have a working understanding of what sound actually is. If you're going to change something, or control something, you need to have a clear foundation of just what *that something* is.

As we move through the rest of this chapter, you might not pick up on 100% of the concepts that we're going to go over. Don't worry about it, that's okay. What's important is that you are exposed to these concepts. Many of them may only make sense to you in the future after something or someone else presents it to you in a way that makes it all click. Take in what you can now, trust me, you'll never stop learning these concepts.

When I say sound, you'll have a basic understanding of what I'm talking about, but you won't necessarily think of it in terms of what it actually is, so let's begin to dissect and break down our craft, so we can reconstruct it and rebuild it in later chapters.

The Medium
Controlling sound is an art. Every artist will have a medium that they work within in regard to their particular art form. If you are a painter, for instance, your tools will be your paint brushes and oils, and your medium will be the canvas on which you paint and create.

Before any artist can create a stunning work of art, he must study and learn about his medium. A painter, for instance, will understand how his paints will soak into and interact with his canvas as opposed to an ignorant person who decides to paint on a plank of wood. Unless you understand your medium on an artistic level, your results will always be mediocre at best.

The discipline of sound reinforcement is no different. In sound, our brushes are our microphones, and our tools are our control surfaces. The medium that we create on, or rather in, is air.

When you're teaching someone to paint, it's easy enough to show them a canvas. They will have an easel with a boxed canvas that they can touch, hold, and examine. Unfortunately, air is invisible to us. We cannot see it with our eyes, nor hold it in our hands. We know when it is present because we are able to breathe. We can see its affects, but we can have a difficult time picturing just what air is, and because of that, it can be difficult to understand precisely what we are doing with our medium as sound engineers. To better understand what we are doing, let's look at another familiar medium that has similar characteristics, but this time, characteristics that we can see. Let's look at a body of water.

Both water and air are made of molecules. Both mediums actually react quite similarly to stimulus and affect. When we look at our body of water, free of stimulus, we see it at rest. It is a smooth surface, like a sheet of glass. Now we'll take a small rock, and drop it into our body of water. As our rock hits the surface, it causes a dent as it enters it. This pushes up water into a peak that causes a chain reaction in a circular pattern in our body of water. This pattern of crests (high points) and troughs (low points) emanate from the point of entry for the rock and travel outward, dissipating at a predictable rate for the medium as the water molecules crash into each other, eventually slowing back down to a point of rest. A surfer understands the power of these waves and uses them in a way that will propel him through the medium.

The same thing is happening in sound when a stimulus happens in the air. A stimulus can be anything that causes a sound. When a stimulus occurs, at its point of emanation, it will cause air molecules to crash into one another and it starts a similar chain reaction to the one we see in the water. In their normal state, these molecules are more or less randomly evenly spaced throughout the medium. However, when they are pushed, they will bunch up and begin to crash into one another, being accelerated in a direction away from its initial stimulus. The places where the crashing or bunching occurs can be likened unto the peak of the water wave, the space or void created in these waves can be likened unto the dip or the valley of the water wave. Depending on the stimulus, these waves will travel through the air with varying rates, or what we refer to as *frequency*.

Gotta Tell Stories

In nature, these molecules bunch up to cause the peak of the wave and create an area of vacuum between. This momentum propels the sound wave out from the source. This happens predictably, mathematically, and somewhat orderly. There is one instance that I can think of where this phenomenon does *not* occur orderly, and when it happens, the result is observable and devastating.

When we mess with the rules of the game, we can create unnatural situations with horrible outcomes. One such way that you will be familiar with is in the case of an atomic explosion. We've all seen the videos of atomic weapons with their devastating destructive power and ensuing mushroom cloud. But what exactly is happening there with sound?

With an atomic explosion, a tremendous force is unleashed in an instant. The force is so powerful, that it pushes the air molecules out of the way so fast that it doesn't leave enough time for the molecules to recoil into a negative waveform. You're left with a positive wave blast that leaves no negative in its wake which breaks the rules of the program. When no negative is present, a void is formed, almost as destructive as the original blast itself. This void creates a vacuum in its wake and nature abhors a vacuum Anything and everything within the blast zone is sucked up into this super-heated vacuum, producing the ever familiar mushroom cloud.

A relatively small amount of people have actually heard a nuclear blast and have lived to describe the sound. Almost all of the archival footage that we see from the newsreels have a conventional blast overdubbed on the film footage. The sound is not from an atomic explosion at all. Those who have heard one describe it as a loud crack followed by an eerie unnatural low-frequency growl that goes on for a long time as the heat and cloud rises.

These waves and patterns *are* very predictable however in God's creation when man has not tampered with them. They are measurable and mathematic from the lowest of frequencies to the highest. Low frequencies are very long, measuring many feet in distance, just to complete a single cycle. High frequencies are very short and close together.

Sound frequencies below twenty cycles per second can actually be seen and counted sometimes with the naked eye if circumstances are just right. This occurred to me once on October 17, 1989. On that day I was sitting in my home office in the basement of my house. My three-year-old daughter was peacefully sleeping in her bed upstairs. At 5:04 PM I began to feel a low-frequency vibration and shortly after began to see the sheetrock walls of my office begin to move in and out at around four cycles per second. Because I was underground, I was treated to a unique view of the Loma Prieta earthquake as it swept through the Northern California Bay Area.

The experience was almost silent underground. The science guy in me would have liked to have stayed there, watching the rolls of energy move through the earth, but the realistic side of my brain wasn't fond of the idea of possibly becoming entombed in the process, so I headed up the stairs to my daughter's room.

It was only after coming up the stairs that I was able to then hear the power of the quake. Now I was able to hear the groaning of the timbers of the house and the clacking of the concrete slabs on my porch as I headed outside with a semi-awake startled daughter.

Frequency
Frequency is simply the amount of times something happens within a set amount of time. My Starbucks frequency in a given week is three.

* * *

With sound we measure the frequency of a sound by how many times a sound wave completes a cycle from ground zero on a graph, to its peak, then through its zero point down to its equal negative position, then returns to baseline zero. This is one cycle. We then measure how many times the sound wave completes that cycle in one physical second of time, to determine its frequency. If a tone completes the cycle 1000 times in a second, then the frequency of the tone is 1000 cycles per second or 1000 CPS. In the 1930s we named this convention of measurement after Heinrich Rudolph Hertz, a German physicist who was the first to conclusively prove the existence of electromagnetic waves in the 1800s. The unit of Hertz is commonly abbreviated as Hz, so a 1,000 Hertz tone is stated as 1 kilohertz or 1 kHz.

Amplitude

In sound, we commonly refer to the act of making something louder as amplification. Guitarists play through amplifiers and we use amps to power public address loudspeakers. In consoles and processors, the electronic signal of the sound is amplified on a micro level through electronic chips known as operational amplifiers or op-amps for short. Sound is transformed into an electronic impulse at a micro level by way of a microphone.

In reference to a sound wave, what all these devices are doing is increasing the amplitude of the sound wave. The amplitude of the wave is the height of the crest and the depth of the trough of the wave. As amplitude increases, so does the distance between the top and bottom of the wave. We perceive this as loudness.

We measure loudness in the form of decibels. Its basic meaning refers to a measurement that refers to a tenth of a bell. The bel in the word decibel honors telecommunications pioneer Alexander Graham Bell who is generally credited with inventing the first commercially viable telephone. Bell also went on to found the *American Telephone & Telegraph Company*. You may know the company better as AT&T.

* * *

The Decibel, or dB, is a comparative form of measurement. That is to say, dB is not the same as an inch. An inch is always an inch, and you can plainly see a line that is an inch long. By contrast, dB is a unit of measurement that is comparative and logarithmic in nature. For instance, you can relate that a sound is 3 dB louder than another at the same frequency. We can determine the threshold of hearing, for instance, assign a dB value to it, and then use a comparative scale to measure other sounds by it.

Generally speaking, when it comes to human hearing, with every 3 dB of gain that is added, the perceived loudness of a sound doubles. So if I am listening to a loudspeaker at 100 dB, if I make it twice as loud, I am now listening at 103 dB. That is why there is a world of difference between a worship team rocking at 103 dB, and a rock concert at 106 dB.

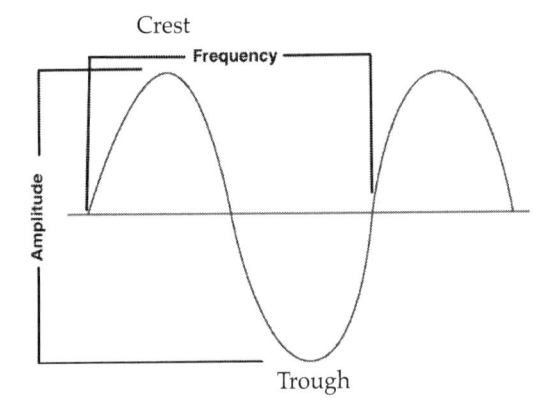

Chapter 4

Sound Science

Gardening 101

I love gardening. There's just something about a well-kept yard that's incredibly rewarding. I take pride in my backyard, and over the years it has become an oasis for my wife and me, a place to relax and perhaps share a dinner at the end of a stressful day. Now I know that you're asking yourself what does gardening have to do with sound science? You can be sure that I'm about to tell you.

In the previous chapter, we took a simple look at sound. In this chapter, we're going to start to look at reality. If every sound and every tone was mathematically pure and simple, we'd have a really easy job as engineers. Unfortunately, that one dimensional way of looking at sound is simply not reality. Sound is incredibly complex, and there is no such thing as a *pure sound* in this fallen world. Instead, sound is riddled with artifacts and distortions of the truth, slight imperfections that alter the purity of its original design. Why is this?

Adam was the original gardener on planet Earth, and I'm guessing he was a pretty good one. But after the fall, nature was somehow infected by the sin that entered in by way of Adam and Eve. His job as a gardener was no longer easy. It was now an uphill fight to get his garden to grow as it once did. Thorns and weeds came in and fought his efforts at every turn. After the fall, I'm sure Adam could still picture that perfect garden in his head, and for the rest of his days, I'm sure he strived to get his garden to be as close to that picture as it could, but there was a barrier to perfection now. A stubborn weed that could not be killed. It would come back time and time again. His building blocks where now imperfect, and when he tried to build a perfect garden, those flawed building blocks would always creep back in at every opportunity.

Today technology keeps coming up with better weed killers and better gardening tools, but the funny thing about it is that the better we get, the more it points us back to the reality that we can't get back to that perfection that once was. In a sense, as it relates to what *once was*, the angel is still guarding the gate to that garden. We are always reminded that the best we can do now, is the best we can do. Not perfection, but compromise.

Like gardening, sound is all about compromise. Adam had to learn the hard lesson of what it meant to *get it as good as he could*. He soon learned the harsh reality of the effect that natures new imperfections would play on his garden. In sound, we also must come to a point of realizing the imperfections in nature that exist that make our challenge every bit of an uphill battle so we can do our best to work with and around those challenges to get the very best compromised result that we can. In this chapter and the few that follow, we'll be looking at the various challenges, shortcomings, and sciences behind sound and how we perceive it.

Over the next few chapters, it may sound initially like I'm repeating myself from time to time, but that's really not the case. We will be going over terms like phase, frequency, and others time and time again. Each time we'll look at just a slightly different dimension of the term, and how it affects us. The more we understand the multidimensionality of what we're dealing with, the more we will understand how to control it. I'm going to show you things in the next few chapters from a number of different angles, and in a sense, we're going to place those things on a table and walk around it. We're going to see these concepts as objects, to be looked at from many different views.

Phase
Sound is anything but simple. The first characteristic we'll be looking at is phase. Like dB, phase is another comparative term. It refers to the comparative points in a given cycle of two waves, or

simply the starting point of a wave. In other words, if a sound wave starts at one point in time from point A and travels to point B by means of two paths, those waves may recombine out of perfect phase at point B as they arrive at point B after traveling in two different directions. If our sound creates two simple waves and one travels from point A to point B directly, it may not arrive at point B in phase with wave 2 that takes a more indirect path, perhaps one that reflects off a wall, then arrives. The two signals may arrive at point B completely out of phase or any number of degrees out of phase for that matter.

The takeaway here is to be aware that this phenomenon is happening in a myriad of ways as you are manipulating sound. This is why a sound will sound different throughout a room. As waves reach places in time close to or approaching 180 degrees out of phase, they will theoretically cancel each other out. As others arrive totally in phase, or close to it, they will theoretically cause summation and increase in volume. I say theoretically because there really is no such thing as a perfect pure tone.

Sooner or later, you'll be in the middle of a perfect soundcheck or service, with everything flowing beautifully, and out of nowhere, something will let loose and go into feedback. What was that? You'll sit up, eyes and ears wide open, wait for it to happen again, but it won't. What is that when that happens? That is momentary summation. At a given place and time, two tones happen simultaneously, in near perfect phase, at a select frequency, causing the said frequency to momentarily push itself over your feedback threshold. An ever so brief freak summation of like frequencies. The perfect storm if you will.

Most of the time we can only drop a little of that frequency out of the offending input or entire mix and hope for the best. The lesson here is that sound is not static or one dimensional. It is in a constant state of change and there is a myriad of factors in your medium and environment that you must take into account.

* * *

There are a few things that you can do to minimize the negative effects that phase can play on your mix. The most basic is to be sure that all of your speakers are in phase with each other to begin with. If a speaker cabinet has one or more drivers wired out of phase with the rest of the system, that speaker will cause sound cancellation. This is the most prominent with low-frequency speakers.

If you have a left and right sub, and one of those boxes has its plus and minus terminals reversed, it will almost completely cancel out the sound that they are trying to reproduce. As you walk back and forth between those speakers, you will hear the sound dropping in and out and *phasing* as you vary the amount of phase cancellation by varying your listening location. If you correct the wiring, good low-end will return, not perfect low-end mind you, but good low-end that at least starts with its two original source points in phase with one another.

If you have more than two subs in a system, let's use four for an example, and one is wired out of phase, the result will be much harder to hear. This situation will generally result in an overall decrease in low-frequency efficiency in the entire system.

Today's modern bi-amped and tri-amped speakers will actually vary phase in their processing to use phase to their advantage. They might run a midrange driver slightly, (or totally for that matter) out of phase with a low-frequency driver in order to phase cancel some frequencies at the crossover point in order to knock down a frequency that is too hot.

We can also do many things with microphone technique to minimize potential phase issues when mic'ing instruments and vocals. We'll delve into those techniques later in the chapters that deal with technique specifically.

Harmonics
In a poetic sense, it can be said that music is the language of God. On the surface, we perceive music in an analog manner, a

blend of tones working with each other to produce a string of sounds that are pleasant to our brains. Good music can affect our mood and move us emotionally and spiritually.

In a mathematical sense, we can begin to see and understand this *language of God* in a literal way. Below the surface, music is anything but analog. It is a quantized digital programming language with measurable, predictable mathematic quantizations that we commonly call harmonics.

Picture it this way. I am writing a book on a computer. I'm using an advanced program to write that book that responds to my typing. Every time I clunk down on a key on the keyboard, I'm not thinking about the ones and zeros that it took in the digital domain for a programmer to build this program that is allowing me to write this book. I'm not thinking about the compiler, or the operating system of the computer, or any of the other processes going on under the surface of my flowing analog experience. Instead, I am enjoying the fluidity of the program in a natural analog way.

When it comes to engineering sound, unlike the common listener, we cannot ignore the programming language under the surface. We must be constantly aware of it, understand it, and use it to help shape what we hear.

Harmonic tones are found in virtually all sound. They are frequencies embedded in the original sound at predictable mathematically placed intervals, at predictable mathematically assigned volumes. They are digital in the sense that these steps are found at predictable quantized intervals throughout all sound. As we begin to dissect how this works, in the back of your mind you should be asking the simple question, "Is this evidence of random chance, or is this evidence of programming and engineering?"

To break this down, we are going to start with a simple 1000 Hz tone. If I had a tone generator and played a 1K tone through a PA system, your brain would perceive that tone as a simple sound.

Below the surface however, there would be many more tones, masked by the loudest tone, or what we call, the *fundamental frequency*.

Contained within our simple 1K tone, we would also find a harmonic placed mathematically at double the frequency and again at every interval of that frequency. That is to say that a 1K tone will contain a theoretical tone at 2K, approximately 3dB down in volume from the fundamental. This formula can be tracked predictably throughout the hearing spectrum, at the same quantized intervals, and at the same mathematical dissipation rates, so in our example, we would expect to find a tone at 3K, 6dB down, and 4K Hz at 9dB down, and so on.

These formulas are incredibly important to understand and will be a game changer for any soundman who embraces the physics of them for the first time by realizing how these frequencies all interact. It's literally impossible to do something to affect a frequency, without that change affecting others. We will be going into how this head knowledge will affect your real-world mixing in the next chapter, so don't let it go by as simple science guy blah blah blah.

Notice that I'm using words like theoretical and approximately. Again, we find that this formula is not absolutely perfect. It is so near perfect however, that it does cause one to wonder just what has gone wrong. How can it be so near perfect, so predictable, yet contain the slightest traces of imperfection, just enough to assure that we will never be in a place of perfection? Flaws are inevitable as long as we continue to work within the limitations of our current program. Interesting isn't it?

* * *

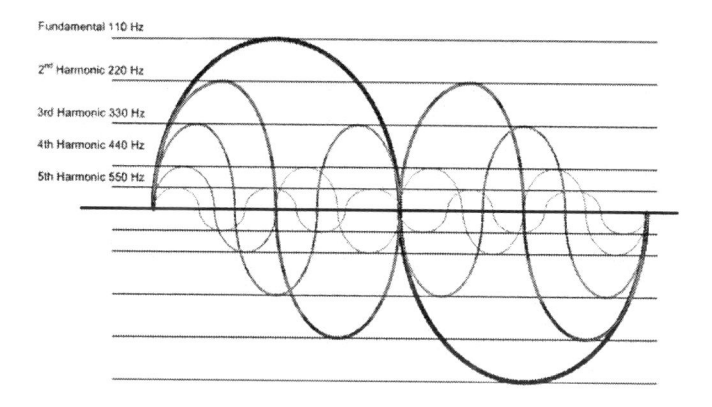

Fundamental 110 Hz
2nd Harmonic 220 Hz
3rd Harmonic 330 Hz
4th Harmonic 440 Hz
5th Harmonic 550 Hz

Distortion

As long as we're looking at imperfections, let's touch on distortion. As the term implies, distortion is any altering of the original sound. We may all know what distortion sounds like, but what does it look like? Let's go back to our original sound wave.

Our wave has a nice round hump and dip. The peak of both hump and dip determines the amplitude of the wave. But what if something unnatural occurs? What if the amplitude exceeds the limitations of the wave? For instance, what if something drives the signal louder than what a piece of electronics can reproduce? The frequency stays the same, but the top and bottom of the wave will begin to get smashed or cut off as the amplitude exceeds the capability of the electronics. At first, it just affects the peaks, the very top and bottom of the wave. We may not hear the distortion at this early stage of the clipping of the wave, but as the rounded nature of our wave continues to flatten out, or distort, the sound will get grittier and grittier as the rounded wave resembles more of a square than a hump.

This is why a console will have a light that tells you when the wave peak is beginning to clip. We commonly refer to these as peak lights or clip lights. It is also where the term *square wave* comes from.

* * *

The Beauty of Design

It has always seemed funny to me that some sound engineers go to such great lengths to tune sound systems flat. That is to say, all frequencies behaving evenly throughout the audio spectrum. The reality, however, is that we do not perceive sound in a flat manner.

The good engineer understands that it's more important to tune a system to be musical. Although humans can generally hear sounds from about 20 Hz on the low end out to about 20K Hz on the high end for those with perfect hearing, we are designed with a bump in the frequency response of our ears from 1,000 Hz to 6,000 Hz. What accounts for this?

To understand why this likely is, we have to ask the question, what would be so important in that specific range that our Creator might have tuned our ears to hear? The answer is simple. The ability to communicate. As it turns out, human speech falls exactly into the very same frequency tuning of our ears. It is a simple truth, but probably not something we consider every day.

Chapter 5

The Medium

So far we've only looked at the basic properties of sound itself, the basic building blocks of sound as it moves through the air. But the air itself is actually part of the whole when we consider sound. The condition of the air in an acoustical space will have a profound effect on the sound that is being produced in that space, whether your space is a room, a chapel, an auditorium, or even the great outdoors. A painter may paint the same exact picture on two different canvases, but if one canvas is a dirty brown and the other is a brilliant white, he will in fact end up with two different pictures, even if he was painting them both simultaneously.

Did We Go to the Moon?

Sound waves differ from radio waves in more ways than simply being lower in frequency. Radio waves are electromagnetic. Because of this, they do not require a medium to move through in order to exist. Sound waves, as opposed to radio waves, are mechanical energy and as such, they require a medium. This is why we can send a TV signal or radio wave to the moon and back, yet if we were to speak to another person in the vacuum of space, they would not hear us, even if they were standing only a few feet away.

A popular argument for those who believe that the moon missions were fabricated, is that they believe that radio waves could not move through the vacuum of space. The particular argument, like many of the others, is born of ignorance and a lack of understanding when it comes to the physics of electromagnetic fields. We routinely listen to electromagnetic fields every day from a multitude of sources coming from deep space, distances far greater than simply sending a signal to the moon, a relatively short distance away.

* * *

The argument can be quickly shot down by physically demonstrating that electromagnetic fields can move through solid objects without the need of a medium. Electromagnetic waves are a form of radiation, so they are more closely likened to light than sound. In fact, they even move at the same relative speed as light itself. If one of these people ask you to prove your theory, simply walk into the next room and call them on your phone. The only thing needed for radio frequencies to travel through space is time.

Humidity

I am a California native. I grew up in California and learned how to engineer sound here. I never ventured outside of my state to mix sound until I was doing sound as a professional engineer. If you live in Atlanta Georgia you will laugh at anyone from California who complains about humidity in our state. Out here on the West Coast, we have no idea what humidity is.

For me, the concept of humidity affecting sound moved out of the realm of the theoretical into the practical the first time I headed out to Georgia to work on a musical with the rest of my family. Just about everyone on my mother's side of the family is involved in theatre and production in some way. I am but one of three sound engineers in the family to put it in perspective.

The particular musical I went out to work on was production of Disney's Cinderella. This was a theatrical event that was to take place in an outdoor amphitheater about a half hour's drive south of Atlanta Georgia. I had body mics on many of my principles, but the majority of the chorus and dialogue mic's from the rest of the cast came from four pressure zone microphones placed across the front of my stage.

At sound check, the ambient temperature in the amphitheater was around 89 degrees. I remember pushing the system pretty hard to get everything I could out of the PZM microphones. I had been in 89° heat doing outdoor shows routinely in my home state of

California, but in Georgia, 89° felt like 105 to a California boy.

Nonetheless, we finished our sound check and had everything dialed in and ready for the first show which was that very night. We all packed up and went out to dinner feeling pretty good about where we were, all set and ready for showtime. When we got back that night the ambient temperature had dropped about 10° and the humidity dropped with it. I remember climbing back behind my board and unmuting my microphones to make sure that everything was still working through my PA before opening doors. When I hit the mute button on the PZM microphones the PA system took off with an incredible feedback howl. What had just happened? The answer to the question, of course, was *physics*.

That day I learned a graphic lesson of how important your medium is when running sound. At soundcheck, I was pushing sound through a different medium. That medium was mostly water. When I returned after dinner, my median was mostly air molecules. Nothing in the Sound system changed. Nothing in the sound pressure levels changed. The only thing that changed was the medium itself. Ask anyone who does sound in the South routinely, and they will assure you that air is thinner than water.

How much thicker was this air at soundcheck? Well, in order to stop everything from feeding back I had to pull all of the faders on my board back about 50%. Touring sound engineers are well aware of this phenomenon in different parts of the country and are faced with the compensation process between soundcheck and show, nightly. If you are a sound engineer in the parts of the country that deal with extreme humidity, you will be forced to take it into account in order to effectively run sound, especially outdoors.

Temperature
Two variations of temperature will affect your sound in major ways, ambient temperature and absorbed or radiated temperature. Ambient temperature is the relative temperature of the air that is all around us in the space we are mixing in. Absorbed or radiated

temperature is the temperature of surfaces in our space and our equipment.

As the ambient temperature heats up, sound speeds up. No, not enough to actually hear, but temperature *will* affect your overall sound. Temperature takes its place alongside things like humidity in the overall influence of thermodynamics in your world of sound.

I've had numerous pieces of equipment over the years simply stop working from heat exhaustion. Everything has a working temperature and if you push things beyond those limits or expose them to excessive heat, they will give up. I have had dimmer packs that refuse to operate during the day and as the sun goes down begin to dim lights, just in time! I have had the main processors on equipment go down after the completion of sound check and have had to be cooled down before the show could even start.

You might say to yourself, "Well that doesn't really apply to me because everything we do in our church is indoors." Actually, the same problems can arise from heat being transferred from certain pieces of equipment in close proximity to other gear, such as when gear is mounted in racks. This is why it's a good practice to always have space in between power amplifiers or any other device that creates heat. On larger installations with multiple amplifiers, we even spec air conditioning units in tech rooms to keep gear cool.

Probably the most overlooked place where temperature affects the operation of your system is in the operator himself. When temperatures go up, your effectiveness to think goes down. Running sound is just as much mental as it is physical. Never underestimate the extreme importance of keeping the sound engineer cool while mixing indoors or out. Obviously outdoors has the greater potential for heat exhaustion in the engineer. This is why we routinely cover the FOH (front of house) mix by means of pop-up tents whenever we do an outdoor show, not just on hot summer days, but always.

* * *

Gotta Tell Stories

I can recall one summer when we had a particularly high heat wave go through the valley in Northern California. On that particular weekend, we had two major outdoor shows for which we were providing sound systems in my hometown. I had four stages running with crews at what was at that time, one of California's single largest one-day festival event. At this particular event, my crews would do about 80 band changeovers in a single day.

At the same time, I was in an adjoining city running a large outdoor heavy metal festival at the local rodeo grounds. We had taken many precautions to keep all of our crew members as cool as possible. I may have been at the rodeo grounds, but it was not my first rodeo when it came to doing hot outdoor shows. At every stage at every event, we had placed a window air conditioner on top of our control racks at the front of house. During the day our engineers could get a mix up and then turn to the left and lay on top of an air conditioner unit as the temperatures rose to 114 degrees. We also had buckets of ice water that were used to soak rags and towels that would then be placed over our crew's heads and necks. The festivals themselves provided no such provisions for their crew members and both festivals had crew people taken away in ambulances due to heat exhaustion while our company suffered no such issues.

I can recall my wife calling me at one point to ask what the two flashing dashes meant on our air conditioners. I looked at mine and saw that I was getting a double dash code on my readout as well. I didn't give it much thought and simply said that I didn't know. About 12:30 AM the next morning as we began breaking down our stages for the load-out, the AC units began to flash 99.

Wind.

There is no greater force out there that will alter your medium than wind. To better understand and illustrate this, imagine being a painter and having your medium spun in place as you're trying to paint on it. To a large extent, that's exactly what's going on when we are trying to mix sound in a windy environment. One of the toughest challenges you will ever face as a sound engineer is mixing sound outdoors on a windy day. You might be saying to yourself, *well fortunately for me that will never affect me, because I'm always mixing sound indoors at my church.* Guess again.

Wind is a naturally occurring process through thermodynamics that stirs the air. We have figured out ways to accomplish the same thing indoors artificially. It's called air conditioning! Air conditioners are the biggest friends, and at this same time, the biggest enemies of sound engineers and lighting designers. It really is a love/hate relationship. On the upside, they can make you comfortable in a room. There are few things worse than sweating away over a sound console. Engineering is a skill best practiced in comfort.

On the downside, you have an environmental system that is fighting you every inch of the way. It is changing the temperature in your room so you are constantly having to change what you are doing with your mix. It's moving air back-and-forth in your room so your medium is constantly being stirred. It's taking the sound in the room and pulling it towards air conditioning returns continually so it is in effect redirecting your sound continually.

Not all frequencies in the hearing spectrum will be affected in the same way when it comes to wind. High frequencies are much more fragile and delicate than lower frequencies. High frequencies can be fractions of an inch long, while bass frequencies can be many feet in length. A 60 Hz tone is just shy of twenty feet in length. So if you can picture in your mind a keyboardist hitting a low B around 60 Hz, that note is going to go through a complete cycle about once every nineteen feet. By contrast, a cymbal on a drum kit might produce a 14K sound that is less than an inch in length. These high frequencies are incredibly delicate and are greatly affected by any movement in the medium.

Now bear in mind that we don't have to spend an exorbitant

amount of money to come up with an environmental system that will screw up our sound. It can be accomplished in the simplest of unintentional ways. I remember going to a church once to give a sound seminar. All of the sound engineers in the church began relating to me their woes of how hard it was to mix in the particular room. They would tell me that there were times that it was much harder than others and they really didn't understand why. I asked them if there was any particular time of year in which it was more difficult. They looked at each other and said, "Well yes, come to think of it, the summertime is much more challenging than the winter." I just looked at them with a smirk on my face and slowly looked up at the twelve large hanging fans in the sanctuary. After a few seconds, one of the engineers sheepishly said, "Oh."

Altitude

Altitude is another factor to take into consideration when mixing sound. The greater your altitude, the slower your sound will tend to travel. Again this is not something you're going to necessarily hear, but it needs to be something you're aware of as it will have a definite effect on your sound. I don't bring all of these factors to your attention because there is a long list of *dos and don'ts* when it comes to mixing sound at different altitudes or different temperatures, but rather to drive home the point that there are many factors at play that you need to take into account when you are mixing a room or a venue.

If you're doing traveling sound with something like a choir tour or your worship team and you have a digital console on which you've saved your show file, know that that file is simply a starting point for when you get to your next venue, because the next time you get into a different environment all of these key things will change. This is why it's just so funny for a sound engineer to walk into a church and see a piece of tape on something in the sound room that says, "Everything sounds great, don't change anything!" The reality is, that your environment will change and things will sound different every day, sometimes in small ways, sometimes in huge ways. Mixing sound was never intended to be an idle pursuit.

***

The Path Less Traveled
So far we've only been talking about sound moving through the medium of air, but there are other paths through which sound will travel within an environment. Have you ever been sitting in your house and heard a car drive by with a loud stereo? What exactly did you hear when it passed? Did you hear great highs inside your house? Chances are what you heard were the lowest frequencies making their way into your living room. This is because low frequencies like to travel through hard flat surfaces.

Many churches will go to great lengths to make sure that their foyers are closed off acoustically from the sanctuary. However, even when the doors are closed you will find that the low frequencies from the main room are creeping out into the foyer. This is because those frequencies are traveling through the ground rather than the air, passing right into the next room.

Recording studios will go to great lengths to actually float rooms so this path is broken. They will float a floor in a room by setting it on sand, making sure that there is an inch or so space between one floor in one room and the floor in the adjacent room.

Another body that sound will travel across is water. I once knew an engineer who invented a sub speaker enclosure that operated on the premise of vibrating a water bladder mechanically instead of moving a speaker to push air. Low-frequency waves would travel out from his sub along hard surfaces until they encountered something else made of water. Once the frequencies found *something* made of water they would vibrate that *something* at the same frequency that they were vibrating at themselves.

You've probably already guessed what that *something* was. Of course, I am talking about human beings. We are made of mostly water, and our rib cages are the bodies receptor of the lowest of frequencies. I had the opportunity to take a couple of his prototypes out into the real world of professional audio one summer to do the pro-audio phase of his beta testing. On one event we did an outdoor show with his sub enclosure on an island in the middle of a small lake. Essentially this single box turned the entire lake into a low-frequency driver. Houses over a mile away were reporting that they were feeling low end as if they were sitting at the concert.

There has never been a device so small that has had the ability to throw sub frequencies for such great distances with little to no degradation. It would have revolutionized the large-scale outdoor concert industry by providing exacting low-frequency sound to every body in the house perfectly and evenly. It would have revolutionized the car stereo industry by allowing the passengers inside the car to experience low frequencies as clean and as loud as they wished, with total isolation to the outside world because of the tires rubber isolation to the ground. Imagine sitting in a car with the loudest rap music your body could take, pounding you away with low frequency. Then opening the door and stepping out of the car with the low-frequency portion of the sound immediately stopping.

It was a genius idea. Why didn't the idea ever make it into the world of professional sound? He eventually sold the patent to a large speaker manufacture and electronics designer that literally sat on the technology in order to bury it. The products that they manufactured were in direct competition with this device and they were too short-sighted to see how this could revolutionize the industry. That's the way the business world works sometimes folks.

Chapter 6

Rings, Feedback, and Other Things That Drive You Nuts

What is Feedback?

When you use the term feedback, people generally know what you're talking about. That loud obnoxious sound that occurs when something is too loud. Technically feedback occurs when a microphone picks up a sound that has already been amplified through a system and amplifies it again, over and over. This produces a feedback loop of the original sound and generates the classic feedback howl at the loudest offending frequency.

The best thing about feedback is that feedback will generally tell you what frequency is causing it. If you have a howl occurring at 800 Hz, then generally dipping out that offending frequency will stop the feedback from occurring. I used the word generally because you also must consider the harmonics of an offending frequency as well.

If you're a visual learner rather than a conceptual learner, you can visualize this phenomenon by holding up a mirror to another mirror. This exercise will produce a visual feedback of the reflected signal.

What Are Rings?

Rings, like feedback, are frequencies that are looping back through the system, however, in this case, there is insufficient volume for them to regenerate more than a few times. The result is the sound of something *wanting* to feedback. There are few things more distracting during a service or event than a constant drone of something wanting to let go.

* * *

When you're faced with a ring in your system, the first order of business is to determine the source of it. Sometimes it will be obvious, other times it will be more difficult to locate. Many times it will be the product of two or more things interacting with each other. As you run these offending frequencies down, you must think multi-dimensionally. Simply turning one thing down may not be enough to solve your problem. Take as many things into account as you can to determine the cause and solution to your issue. Take into account mic placement, the original sound of the instruments, the amplified sound of the instruments, and the interaction of the instruments with one another in the mix.

Good mic placement is always your first line of defense with rings. A properly placed mic will stop a ring before it ever has a chance to become an issue in the first place. Vocal mics, for instance, are designed to reject sound entering from the back of the mic, so place vocal mics in such a manner that they are at an opposing angle to the wedge at your feet in order to achieve maximum rejection. The hardest placements to achieve this will be with keyboardists, as you'll almost always need to come in from the side with the wedge, so be creative, and get maximum rejection where you can. If you have a singing drummer, don't place his wedge firing into his mic.

What's Happening With Volume?
When one thinks about the causes of feedback, the natural default is to blame volume. If something is feeding back in a PA speaker or monitor, then it's simply too loud, right? The simple answer is that it could be, but the reality of sound is that overall volume is but one simple factor when it comes to feedback, and feedback causality is often a complex matter.

For instance, with proper engineering, you can engineer a stage monitor to be very loud and still not feedback, even to the point where a performer can point a microphone directly into it without feedback. You can engineer a house PA so a person with a mic can walk directly in front of it, so clearly volume is not the only consideration.

* * *

When it comes to volume and feedback, we're really looking at frequency-specific volume as opposed to overall signal volume. This is where the balancing act of compromise comes into play. On one end of the spectrum, you can EQ a signal to sound full and rich with no regard for frequencies that might feedback. On the other end of the spectrum, you can hack up a signal so severely, that there's just nothing left to actually feedback. As with all things in sound, balance is the order of the day, and there will be a compromise somewhere in the middle that will allow a channel to sound good, yet you'll have lost most of the energy in the frequencies that will want to take off. Knowing where that sweet spot is, comes from time and experience.

What's Happening With Phase?
Phase comes into play when two signals combine in a monitor or house mix causing specific frequencies to momentarily double in volume. This can commonly occur in vocal monitors when two vocalists hit the same note in time in near perfect phase with each other, causing a specific frequency to increase in volume and push over the edge of feedback. So in this circumstance is it a volume problem, a frequency problem, or a phase problem? The answer is….Yes.

The longer you work with sound, the better you'll understand these variations on issues, and the more discerning you will become as to which actions to take to remedy various situations as they arise. The more experienced you become with your craft, the more you'll realize the vast amount of tools you actually have at your disposal.

Sometimes, adjustment of the overall volume may be what is needed to fix an issue. Sometimes a phase caused issue might be avoided simply by throwing one of the sources out of phase with the other. Sometimes a surgical approach might be needed to reduce a specific frequency in one or both of the competing sources. Sometimes it is a different combination of each of these solutions.

* * *

The more that you understand the nature and physics of sound, the more you will see your spectrum of options for solutions grow when it comes to controlling and shaping it. Don't be surprised if you come to a point when it puts a smug smile on your face when someone comes up to inform you that some simple solitary thing needs to be done to fix something in the mix. Then again, always listen to your occasional sound helper because let's face it, sometimes the simple observation of, "The guitar is too loud," is correct.

What's Happening With Harmonics?
Harmonics can be one of those irritants that drive you nuts because the little cowards hide. Sound is about controlling what you can hear, *and* what you can't. So how then do harmonics come into play when it comes to causing feedback?

Let's look at a working example of how this might play out in your system. Let's take a brief moment in time when something feeds back at 1K. We might have a vocalist who hits a momentary note with a loud amplitude at 500 Hz. The guitar in the mix also hit a note of louder than normal amplitude at 1K. For that moment, the harmonic in the vocalists signal, because the fundamental at 500 Hz was so strong, might produce a significant tone at 1k, loud enough to couple with the guitars 1K fundamental frequency and cause momentary summation. Bingo! Feedback at 1K is produced. The feedback at 1K in the mix might be avoided by reducing 500 Hz in the vocalist's mic, even though you couldn't hear the 1K tone because it was masked by the fundamental frequency.

The take away is to get to the point where you are thinking multi-dimensionally, taking in as many factors as you can while mixing. Sound is complex, and you might get to the point where you think you're starting to overthink sound, and I guarantee you, you're not. Even the best engineers in the world cannot fully comprehend everything going on in the medium they're controlling. Just don't overthink to the point of becoming paralyzed by the complexity of it. In the end, when something goes wrong, you still have to come up with the best solution that you know to fix it.

What's Happening With Acoustics?
We'll spend an entire chapter here in a bit, but if we're going to be looking at things that drive you nuts, we have to touch on acoustics. Nothing will set the limitation of how good you can make something sound, then the construction of the acoustic space in which you are mixing. The biggest frustration here is that it is what we refer to as a *brick wall limitation*. That means that this limitation will never be overcome. You will never be able to push past the limitation of bad acoustics. There are always things that you can do to maximize how good things sound up to the point that the particular limitation is reached, then it will be impossible to push beyond that barrier.

I have a show that I do every year at a particular fairground. I do this event in an old fairground building with horrible acoustics. For years I used a ground stacked trapezoid point and shoot type PA system. After a few years of doing this event, we eventually went over to a flown line array system in the same room. Though the show still did not sound as good as a show in a great acoustical space, flying the PA did improve the sound of the event. However I have to note, it still did not sound great, *better*, yes, *great*, no. That particular show will never sound great because of the hard limitations of the acoustics.

When faced with poor acoustics you really have to drop back from an artistic mode into a survival mode. The good engineer realizes that at times, this is the best one can hope for. If you allow yourself to become frustrated with poor acoustics when faced with them, you are going to spend your existence behind the board in a very frustrated state. You'll also be wasting your valuable and limited energy fretting over something you can't change. My best advice is to simply understand the acoustics that you're dealing with, do your best to minimize their effects, and understand that it will be your final hard limitation as to how good you will be able to make it sound.

What's Happening With Limitations?

While we're on the subject of limitations, let's look at some others. Limitations are all around us. I have had an opportunity to talk with many sound engineers who become frustrated with the limitations that surround them. More often than not, church budgets will not allow for sound equipment that is of the highest caliber. Often times sound engineers must simply make do with the equipment that has been placed at their disposal.

I'm going to let you in on a little secret here. These same limitations apply to audio at every level, from its cheesiest to its most extravagant. Every arena sound engineer with every major touring artist is dealing with equipment limitations that at times will drive them nuts. Even with the most expensive high-end gear, there are levels and degrees of quality within them. Yes, you may be starting at the bottom of the totem pole, but the plague of limitations will not go away as you climb it.

The more you begin to understand your equipment limitations, and work within them, the more you will be able to have a clear mind that will be able to prioritize the needs of overcoming those limitations and replacing gear that needs to be replaced in the most effective order that you possibly can. The good engineer will always get the best out of what he has to work with, and he will channel his frustration into a prioritized list of what pieces he will concentrate on replacing first in order to make his life, and the quality of sound that everyone hears better.

Ambient Room Noise

As a working sound professional, it never ceases to amaze me when non-sound engineers place house mix positions in noisy environments. I've set up entire systems at festivals and gone to lunch only to return an hour later to find an air compressor running at 102db twenty feet from my mix position keeping a jump house inflated. Even in the serenity of the sanctuary, you will find ambient noise that you will have to deal with, and while it may not be as extreme as our jump house, it can still drive you nuts.

Ambient room noise could include noisy HVAC units, adjacent rooms with noisy spillover such as Sunday School rooms or youth rooms, or simple street noise creeping into your sound mixing environment. There will always be a noise floor whatever your environment may be, but if you find that the noise is excessive or unacceptable, take action where appropriate to minimize these distractions. Actions may be as simple as relocating a mix position, or as complex as taking isolation measures with walls in between offending rooms. Simply assess your situation, and ask yourself if there are any realistic solutions that might be had to at least minimize these distractions for both you, and the congregation.

Equipment Failure
Even with a brand new sound rig, equipment failures happen on a regular basis. As systems become more and more complex, the likelihood of failure increases proportionately. Failures can really drive you crazy as they seldom happen at opportune times. Your best line of defense from equipment failure is two-fold, preventative maintenance, and failure expectation. You have to expect it, be prepared, and plan for it.

When we think of preventative maintenance, we usually think of it in terms of taking care of our house or our car, but there are plenty of areas in our sound systems that with proper maintenance the health and life of that system can be greatly extended. One huge area is in the realm of interconnects. Cables are the arteries of our system through which its electronic lifeblood flows.

Throughout your setup take care to see that there is no tension on any cable at any point. In an audio system, slack is your friend. On professional shows, I can accurately judge the competence and experience of a crew member on setup simply by observing his cable paths and whether his cables are relaxed or taught.

* * *

Your second line of defense is failure expectation and fail-safe planning. When was the last time that you were surprised by a vacation you took when you had been planning it for months? Failure is inevitable. The trick is that it's hard to completely plan for it when you have so many parts to a complete working system and never really know what might fail.

What we *can* do is look at our system and ask ourselves, *what is mission critical? What can't we live without? What are the critical pieces that simply cannot be worked around if they fail?*

One advantage to consider is that when we are running church sound, we are seldom running sound on the churches very first system. That is to say, most churches, clubs, schools, or whatever, are usually in a semi-constant state of upgrade as technology and needs change. This can work to our advantage.

Let's consider the church's console. To a large extent, the console is a piece of gear in the system that is mission critical. If it goes down, you'll have no way to mix a service. So what happens when you finally decide to pull the plug on the poor old 16 channel $800 analog board you've been getting by with and replace it with a shiny new $5000 digital one? The first inclination might be to totally get rid of the old one. After all, the poor tired thing has a few channels that don't even work anymore, and if you simply touch it, your hands stick to it from all the years of tape build up on the scribble strip.

Putting it up on eBay for $25 might not be the best strategy for the old beast. You never know when that retired piece of junk might just have one more service left in it when your shiny three-year-old digital console decides that it won't power on thirty minutes to service.

If you're fortunate enough to run sound at a church with a new fully functional portable sound system for events outside the sanctuary, you'll always have a fallback when things go wrong, but if you don't, you might want to think twice about getting rid of obsolete, yet functional working key pieces. Think of it as cheap insurance.

The Myopic Wife

Does this sound familiar to you? You've just laid out your console and have started your soundcheck. You raise the kick drum channel and you're zoned in on getting that great kick drum tone. Right about the time you move onto the snare, the wife of the bass player runs back to you highly agitated. "Why can't I hear the bass? Can't you hear that you can't hear the bass? The bass isn't loud enough!" "Yes ma'am," You tell her. "I will get to the bass in a moment, right now I'm working on drums."

Yes, I can hear your snickers through the pages of the book. The scenario above is funny because we've all experienced it at one time or another if we do sound. These interruptions can cause frustration on the part of the engineer. Just remember that on any given Sunday, grace needs to be an available tool in your tool bag.

Chapter 7

Garbage In, Garbage Out

We've all heard the saying *garbage in, garbage out*. The saying is especially applicable to mixing sound. I've watched frustrated sound men time and time again at sound checks twisting knobs in an attempt to get something to sound right. For some reason, in our minds, we tend to think that our job begins and ends with that desk in front of us with all of the knobs on it. That could not be further from the truth. Sound starts with the source.

The professional sound engineer knows that he will never be able to effectively improve the sound of an instrument or voice unless the quality is there to begin with. Oh yes, we can affect something with reverb, or stereo-ize a mono signal, or EQ the tonality of an instrument or voice, but we are always simply changing or enhancing what is already originally there.

There are ample things to talk about when it comes to garbage; garbage is everywhere. The first place to consider garbage is in your sound system itself. No, I'm not telling you that your sound system is garbage, but if your sound system is not properly tuned to begin with, you will be starting off with garbage, and it's hard to elevate yourself from that point. Even with a large professionally built sound system, if your sound system is not tuned properly from the very beginning, you will always be starting from a place of garbage, hence, garbage in, garbage out.

Gotta Tell Stories

Years ago my company was providing sound for a large street festival in California. It had multiple stages and I had different engineers on all of them. I was roaming the event on foot making sure that all the areas were going well when I walked up to check in on my main stage.

The stage was up and running, but the engineer seemed to be having a lot of difficulties. I walked up behind him and stood there for a few moments listening and watching what he was doing on the console. My engineer was turning a lot of knobs just to get good tones out of the rig. I was listening to the instruments that were coming off the stage and they didn't sound too bad, so what was going on? I walked up to my engineer and asked him, "How's your day going?"

He responded, "Fine, but it's taking a while to get everything sounding right."

I told him, "That's because your system is not properly tuned yet."

He had been rushed for time that morning and was not able to spend the necessary time required to get the rig properly tuned. Consequently, he fought the sound system all day long, making small improvements to the tuning as he went. After the festival day was over we spent a good 20 minutes properly tuning the system, getting the crossover points perfectly set, and getting the system equalized to the space in which it was operating.

If your sound system is not set up properly to begin with, you will do a lot of twisting on knobs to try to get things into the proper neighborhood. If your system is properly tuned to begin with, you will do far less knob twisting, as you will already be in the neighborhood from the start. In the first scenario, you're trying to compensate for the instruments on stage, the acoustics, and the sound system itself. That's a tall order. In the second scenario, you are no longer fighting the system, and you are dialing with a true representation of what something actually sounds like, without the system adding its own coloration.

Behind the 8 Ball

The first step in setting up your sound rig will be to consider the placement of your speakers and mix location in the venue. Sound itself can create *garbage*, so to speak, as it reflects off surfaces and adds itself back into the original sound field. To minimize this effect we go to great lengths when we fly large sound systems in rooms and arenas to keep sound off of the walls and reflective surfaces, but the concept is every bit as important in a two hundred seat church.

A common mistake that I see is the church with two small PA boxes on stage or on stands, pointing straight at the back wall of the room. This situation will cause what is commonly known as a standing wave. The sound exiting the loudspeaker will bounce squarely off of the back wall and head strait for the stage wall. If the sound is loud enough, the cycle repeats over and over again. Think of a pool table when you hit a ball squarely and directly into a bumper. It will bounce back and forth until its kinetic energy dissipates. The harder you hit the ball, or in our case, the louder the amplitude of the sound, the more bounces or reflections will be created.

Like with the pool table, there is a simple solution that will greatly reduce this effect. Simply angling the left and right speakers slightly in, will greatly reduce this effect as the sound will now be slightly redirected as it reflects. This will also aid in keeping energy off of your side walls in the room. Mind you we're not talking about a huge amount of toe-in on your speakers, you'll want just enough to visually notice, but not so much as to focus that energy back on stage at your front line microphones.

Location, Location, Location

Poor mix location is another common ailment with churches. Often the mix location is an afterthought to the layout of the room space. It should seem obvious to anyone that the sound engineer should be able to actually hear what he is mixing, but that's not always so. Other factors besides ignorance will come in to compete with logic. Other factors like walkways, emergency exits, structural pillars, and a myriad of other factors may come against you in picking the perfect mix location, but the basic need you will have to address in order to have a functional mix location is that you must be able to hear from the space in which you're mixing. I've seen mix locations behind stages, behind glass barriers, in balconies off of the main listening area, and even in other rooms. Oy vey!

The very best mix location in a room is typically centrally located, in the back two-thirds of the room, so you can hear the stereo sound field. As you move away from this location due to logistics and constraints, minimize the number of poor location elements that you'll have to deal with.

If you find yourself in the common arena of compromise, deal with those compromises accordingly. Know that if you are on the back wall, you will not have an accurate representation of what the majority of people in the room are hearing, as you will not be aware of the reflections that are coming off of the said wall. I don't mean to say that sound engineering from this location (or nearly any location in a room) is impossible, but each imperfection will add challenges that will have to be addressed. The first challenge is the knowledge that you will have to walk out into the room to accurately hear what you are doing. A person mixing on a right side wall may very well be able to mix a service from the location, but he must walk out of the sound booth into the sanctuary to know what it actually sounds like in the real environment. He must also walk out into the room in order to hear the stereo separation.

Just a technical note here, if you are faced with a less than perfect mix location, consider a console with Wi-Fi control capability. There are many good inexpensive consoles on the market now that can form a Wi-Fi network simply by plugging in a standard cheap computer router. These consoles will typically have free apps that you can download to a tablet to remotely control your console. This will give you the ability to walk your room and mix from literally any location in it.

* * *

The second step in properly setting up a sound system is simply making sure that the equipment is hooked up properly and operating with the correct initial settings. The following chapter will go into this in detail.

You Are What You Eat

While exploring the *garbage in, garbage out* concept, we need to touch on your diet. Not your personal diet, but the diet of your sound system. *You are what you eat* is just as applicable to your sound rig. Sound systems run off wall provided AC power and often times, it's garbage in, garbage out.

We'll touch on troubleshooting ground loops and such later, but for now, let's simply look at the food that your system eats and the quality of it. First off, make sure there's enough! Everything plugged into an electrical circuit eats its fill of food in the form of voltage and amperage (also measured in wattage). Voltage and amperage have a symbiotic relationship. They are two distinct parts of the same thing. Think of a mountain stream flowing down to an ocean. The water is the voltage. In the United States, we have medium size rivers. Our rivers are 110 volts wide. In Europe, rivers are bigger. They are 220 volts wide. Now the amperage is the force at which the water is flowing. The steeper the rivers descent to the ocean, the more forceful the water will flow. The greater the draw on a circuit or as the amps rise, the voltage will tend to drop. When your voltage drops, your food source drops, electrically speaking.

Voltage starvation will manifest itself in a number of ways. With amplifiers, for instance, you may not have enough energy to deal with hard low-frequency transients like kick drums. You may have great low end to begin with, but your great kick may head to the garbage can if the capacitors in the low-frequency amplifiers cannot recharge fast enough for the next kick hit. The result will be an inconsistent sound in the low end with ever-changing levels. If the voltage is low enough, equipment will stop working altogether. As your voltage drops, you will eventually find the weakest link in your audio chain as one or more pieces will shut down altogether.

* * *

Circuits will tend to have a maximum draw potential that is protected by circuit breakers so the circuit stays within an optimal amperage range, protecting them from the danger of overheating or even catching fire. The problem with thermal breakers is that they will not trip fast unless they are seeing something like a dead short or gross overdraw. A circuit being asked to run at its full capacity continually will rob amps and consoles of the headroom that they need to eat and stay healthy.

This is but one reason to try to keep your sound rig on its own dedicated branch circuits. Another reason is the quality of its food. Other electrical devices on a branch circuit can introduce unwanted electrical artifacts into your food supply that can affect your system. Hums, buzzes, and voltage spikes are only a small sample of things that can go wrong with a contaminated food supply. Anything that has anything to do with heating or cooling is the worst thing for eating your power or introducing artifacts into your electrical path. Keep your sound system mains as far from heaters, coffee pots, electric motors, and any refrigeration as you can. "Can I plug this coffee maker in here next to you?" should always be met with a pleasant smile and a firm, "Sorry, no."

The Fly in the Ointment
Every year we provide production for a large event at a high-end golf course. The client feeds us well at this event, and one particular year we were presented with an incredible steak dinner. The meal was paired with an expensive merlot. As the meal was put in front of us, my sound engineer for the event commented, "This is incredible, they've even given us a great wine to enjoy with our meal this year." Just as he said it, and before he could enjoy any of it, a huge house fly flew directly into his glass with a surprisingly loud plunk, and then proceeded to buzz around the glass before drowning in the wine. My engineer simply stared at his meal in disbelief.

The point of the story is that it only takes one piece of garbage in a sound system to completely spoil it. You can spend a fortune on your speakers and microphones, but if it all runs through a cheap off-brand or low-quality mixer, you will never move past the garbage in the chain.

Lastly, First Things First

Lastly, we'll consider the importance of the source itself. Let's consider two different scenarios. In the first scenario, we are going to take a $9,000 Taylor acoustic guitar and mic in with a $99 Shure SM57 dynamic microphone. Let's bring it up through the PA and get it eq'ed and sounding decent. That was pretty easy.

Now, let's take a $9,000 vintage Neumann tube mic and put it in front of a $39 student guitar. Bring it up through the PA, and try to get it to sound good. What's going to happen? As you might guess, the expensive mic will at best only reveal how truly horrible the $39 instrument is, while the relatively inexpensive middle of the road mic will do an excellent job of amplifying the beautiful instrument.

We have two things to look at in this area, the first is the quality of the instrument itself, the second is the skill level of the person playing it. As you mic up your stage, take notice of the quality of the instruments you are working with. What's the condition of the heads on the drums? Are they new? Are they worn out? Are they in tune? Is the bass rig, or any onstage amplifier for that matter, already buzzing before you've even plugged a direct box into it? This is your opportunity to head off obvious problems before you begin to amplify them.

Chapter 8

Sound System Fundamentals

I've done so much with so little for so long, I can now do anything with nothing at all.

For a long period at the beginning of my career, that was my comical mantra. The usual place that all of us start when doing sound is more or less at the bottom. That is to say, that we all have been in a place where the system is what it is, and we have to make whatever that is work as best it can for whatever we're trying to accomplish with it.

In this chapter, we will be looking at the basic building blocks that make up typical sound systems. While on a typical Friday night I might find myself behind a console in an arena, I am reminded that regardless of a system's size, a sound system has pretty much the same function, whether it arrived in three straight trucks, a semi rig, or was put up as a temporary system in an hour on a Sunday morning for a church service. At the end of the day, all systems share the same characteristics. They exist fundamentally to reinforce sounds that would be lost or hard to understand otherwise.

Reinforcement vs. Amplification

There are two different philosophies regarding sound system amplification. On the small end of the spectrum we have reinforcement. With reinforcement, we are simply looking to amplify sounds that are lost in the listening environment. Reinforcement happens typically in small room and small area applications, where the audience would hear a large portion of the band or sermon even if there was no means of amplification to begin with.

* * *

With reinforcement, as the name implies, we are simply listening to the non-amplified sound initially in order to determine what in fact *needs* to be amplified. For instance, a drum kit may be significantly loud for a given room, and everything else may simply need to be amplified to the same level as the drums. In small churches, amplified instruments may be sufficiently loud on their own without any further need of amplification. If a room is small enough, vocals may be the only thing in need of amplification. The methodology here is to listen to the non-amplified worship set, and simply add the elements that are needed.

Total amplification happens when an area or room is so large that everything needs to be amplified through a sound system. The methodology here is more that of a recording engineer who starts from absolute scratch and builds an entire mix through the PA.

In the church environment, there are hybrid situations where both methods apply simultaneously. For instance, if a church service is being broadcast onto the internet, or into another room, a full mix of everything might be needed for that application, while only a small amount of items might need to be in the mix for the actual room where everyone is seated. In this situation, we might construct an alternative mix on an auxiliary bus for the additional mix. In this circumstance, everything in the room might be mic'ed for the aux mix, but never make it into the main house mix.

Subs on Auxiliary Sends

Another use for aux sends is to create a separate mix for the low-frequency signal that's going to the subs. In this method, we create a post-fader aux mix on our console and dial only the things that actually have very low-frequency material in them to the subs.

Because it is a created mix, it is free of vocals, guitars, and any other item that will muddy the house mix in the low frequencies. The only things getting routed into the subs are the things that we want very low-frequency help with such as the kick, the bass, the keys, music playback, etc. Because the mix is post-fader, unlike monitors, it will raise and lower proportionally as you raise and lower the channel fader of the item that you're sending to that aux.

Digital consoles give us the ability to process the sub aux sends with eq's that only allow low-frequency to pass. We would commonly high pass an aux send for this purpose at around 120 Hz. The big advantages with sub-mixes on aux sends is total control in the low frequency of your system and uncluttered lows as well as highs because of the separation achieved by this method.

Types of Boxes
Church sound systems make up the majority of the installations that my company does in any given year. Because this is the case, I've had the opportunity over the past four decades to work with just about every type of PA box available. I've watched new technologies come and go, and I've learned a great deal about the appropriateness of each of these different systems. Churches and church buildings are not created equal. Not all systems work well for all types of churches. Churches have personalities, just like people. Each church personality will lend itself to a different type of PA box.

In-ceiling speakers, for instance, might lend themselves perfectly to a German Baptist church or Church of Christ facility. Any church where full range music production is not in play may benefit from the control of having speakers directly over the heads of the congregation.

Small churches and small buildings may lend themselves to a small point and shoot box. A small room with well under hundred people in it may get along just fine with two fifteen/horn boxes on speaker stands.

Medium to large churches will take full advantage of modern line array boxes that will minimize lobing and various phase problems throughout the room. A properly engineered line array system will deliver a relatively consistent sound pressure level throughout the room. Line array boxes accomplish this by acoustically coupling to one another. What this means is if you hang a cluster of four or five line array boxes on the side of a stage, those five boxes will acoustically couple with each other and the entire cluster will function effectively as one solitary speaker instead of many. Because there is less interaction between the boxes, they are effectively working with each other instead of against. This is why you will have a more consistent sound with fewer dead spots throughout your auditorium.

The other advantage that these boxes provide is the ability to steer the sound. Manufacturers go to great lengths to design their boxes to throw sound forward in order to minimize the sound coming off the back of the cabinets. This provides greater gain before feedback in the audience and causes less interaction onstage with the PA box itself.

Multi-Amping

A simple solitary amplifier and speaker may work just fine for your telephone or iPad, but once you start amplifying sound in larger areas, that simple method will no longer be sufficient. Most modern systems use some form of multi-amping method to power the rig. In simple terms, multi-amping is simply dividing the frequency sections of the rig into two or more separate amplified sections.

You may have an amplifier running the high frequencies of a system while another amplifier runs the low. You may hear terms like bi-amping or tri-amping, but the fact of the matter is that there can be many divisions in the frequency spectrum when it comes to multi-amping. You may have a system that is indeed a four-way system, or even a five-way, but the theory of all of these systems remains the same. We are simply dividing up the audio spectrum into segments and sending those segments to specific amplifiers and speakers in the system in order to run more efficiently than if one amplifier and type of speaker was required to do it all.

Processors
Multi-amp systems will all run some sort of processor to divide the frequencies up amongst the various amplifiers. There are a wide variety of processors available on the market today, and all of them have various features that will tend to set them apart from the next, but they all have one thing in common and that is that they all divide frequencies amongst amplifiers. In higher-end systems, these processors may be built into the amplifiers themselves and may include tunings specific to the cabinets they are powering.

Stand-alone processors may contain any number of effects that are necessary for sound system setups. They can contain but are not limited to equalizers, compressors, limiters, crossover networks, and gain stages. They have the ability to manipulate phase and do complex routing.

Verify Your Rig
A common mistake is neglecting to verify your rig. Simply put, this means powering the rig on and sending a signal through every mix to verify its correct operation. This basic operation should take place every time you power your rig on.

This can be accomplished by sending pink noise or music playback through every monitor mix and through the mains, one send at a time. Also, remember to check any sub-mixes to cry rooms or video mix feeds. There is a real tendency to overlook this critical step when the same system is used in the same way, every day or every week, but do not become complacent! Know every part of your rig is working properly before your worship team arrives.

Verification is more than just confirming that you have signal to every mix. You're also confirming that every monitor mix is going to the correct position on stage and that the entire mix is working. If you lost a horn in a monitor the previous week, it will show up in the verification process. Never rely solely on your musicians on stage to point out a problem when one arises. Be proactive.

* * *

System Tuning

I've been asked, "What's the best way to tune a PA system?" There are actually many methods out there. Some engineers are married to their real-time analyzer (RTA). Some insist on tuning by ear. My personal preference is to use both. First, make sure your rig is balanced correctly with all of its crossover points. The use of pink noise or familiar music will give you an overall indication if one section needs to be raised or lowered.

Every engineer will have albums on their mp3 player that they know like the back of their hand and use regularly for tuning purposes. An album that is overall flat and well engineered. My personal fallback is Steely Dan's Two Against Nature album, but I work with engineers that I respect every day that use a variety of others. Both Sting and Steely Dan are popular favorites because of the engineering techniques of these artists, but really what you're looking for is something that you know extremely well, that's well crafted, and does not sound cluttered.

Once I've tuned my system, I'll usually come back over and kick up some Michael Jackson to hear the overall tightness and check the low-end ratio. Jackson's tracks are interesting because they're really not flat enough for tuning, but they're incredibly musical and will sound great on a flat system without a lot of EQ tweaking. The track The Way You Make Me Feel is one of my all-time favorites for this purpose, *thank you, Quincy Jones*. The beginning percussion hits also give anyone within earshot fair warning that you're about to do a minute of serious testing. As the track drops in, you'll also get a great feel for the stereo separation in your space.

I'm not big on using an RTA solely for the purpose of actual tuning. A totally flat PA will usually not sound musical. Your ears are still the best piece of tuning gear that you have, but RTAs are great tools for helping you visualize what you're hearing.

Gain Structure

Gain structure is a fundamental concept for every sound system regardless of its size. A proper gain structure can be likened to water flow. Picture if you will the water flow gain structure of the earth itself. In the mountains, snow packs melt into water. This water begins to trickle and form together into small creeks. These creeks flow into rivers and gain momentum as they flow downhill towards their ultimate destination, the ocean. As this water flows it gains in volume, power, and intensity. By the time the river has reached the ocean it has reached its maximum flow and dumps into the larger collective body of water. If this water is restricted anywhere along its path, then its gain structure is compromised, and the water is slowed or stopped. We could use a dam for example.

As sound flows through your console it should be viewed the same way as the flow of water as it approches the ocean. You always want to start off at a certain point and grow in intensity as it flows through your entire system. As a sound starts off at the microphone it is being reproduced on a micro level. By the time that electronic flow has reached your loudspeakers, it is reaching its maximum amplification, being sent to the speakers themselves as their final stage. To best preserve the sound, you will want to avoid setting any dams or restrictions in your signal path.

A bad gain structure will amplify the sound to a certain point and then cut it back or restrict it by turning it down at some stage only to re-amplify it again later. This will compress and add noise to the signal as well as distortion. A proper gain structure is essential for an engineer to properly operate a sound system and get the most out of it.

Phantom Power

Microphones with internal electronics as well as active direct boxes will need to run off of a power source. Some may run off of internal batteries, but most have the ability to run off of phantom power, typically supplied by a switch on your sound console. It gets its funny name from the fact that it shares the signal path with the audio path. As the electronic sound signal travels from the microphone to your console as an AC current, the console piggybacks forty-eight volts DC to the microphone on the same wires. These two signals will not interfere with each other. Think of it as a physical train running from station A to station B on the same rails as a ghost train is running from station B to station A. The ghost train passes right through the material train without either ever knowing of the other's existence.

Interconnects
Audio systems generally use two types of analog interconnect cables. These are balanced and unbalanced. Both methods can use either a quarter inch phone connector or a three-pin XLR connector. A balanced cable will send its audio signal over three internal wires consisting of a positive, a negative, and a ground or shield.

The shield or drain wire protects the audio path from stray radio frequency signals and noise that might interfere with the audio, especially as the length of the cable grows. In radio, we call a long wire attached to an electronic device *an antenna*, and in audio, the same rules of physics apply. We need a way to shield the audio cables from these stray fields, so we envelop them in a shield and then drain those stray signals to the ground of the electronic gear to which the cable is attached.

In the case of an XLR, the connector is wired: pin one ground, pin two positive, and pin three negative. In the case of a quarter inch connector, it is wired: barrel ground, tip positive, and ring negative.

An unbalanced cable will have positive, negative, and ground as well, but in the case of an unbalanced cable, negative will share the wire path with the ground. This sharing of the wire can open up the audio path to interference in some circumstances and generally will not work as well in longer runs. So generally speaking, balanced is the preferred method of interconnect due to its superior electronic characteristics.

* * *

Care must be taken when it comes to an unbalanced phone to phone cable in a sound system as many line level or instrument cables can look outwardly the same as a speaker cable. While a speaker cable will pass audio in a line level interconnect situation, they are very different internally and substituting one for the other can be met with dangerous results. A speaker cable is not shielded, so any stray electronic signals are free to enter the audio path when used in a line level situation.

An unbalanced line level cable is not a large enough gauge to handle an amplifiers speaker output and can actually catch fire when used in this situation. Because a line level cable wraps the hot wire within the shield, it will also induce unwanted capacitance and inductance on the line, causing the amplifier to see an inaccurate impedance load on its output, which can cause damage.

Digital cables are different animals still and come in a variety of types and sizes. They differ from analog in the fact that they carry a digital stream rather than an analog voltage. The same cautions apply here; use the proper cables for their intended purpose. The performance of your system depends on it, and in some cases, even your safety.

Inputs to your sound system can be plugged directly into your sound console, but that can be impractical if your sound console is located fifty feet from the stage in the audience. An analog or digital snake is usually employed to get the signals from the stage to the front of house. When a number of inputs come from a specific place on stage, like from a drum kit, for instance, a smaller sub-snake can be used instead of multiple individual mic cable runs.

Cable Care
There is nothing more basic in your sound system than your cables. Every time that you walk into your room to do sound, you'll interact with your interconnects. Mic cables, speaker cables, and patch cables are the roadways of your system. Cables are the classic

example of, *if you take care of them, they will take care of you*.

How you store your cables is just as important as how you use them. Cables wound improperly are subject to a shortened lifespan due to stress on the connectors and the cable itself.

Reels are a wonderful solution for long continuous cables like digital snakes, but they are a poor choice for things like mic cables. The problem with reels is that they will cause stress at every end of every cable rolled onto the reel. The oldest method of rolling each cable individually is still the best practice.

There are two primary methods of cable stays in use today. One is the classic trick line (Think shoestring) and the other is the Velcro cable strap. Both have advantages and disadvantages. Velcro cable stays allow a cable to be wrapped tightly and will not allow it to come apart in a case. Trick line is inexpensive. Both methods will wear out at about the same rate under general use and will have to be replaced on a regular bases.

My personal favorite is the Velcro, but you'll find just as many professionals who swear their allegiance to the old-school trick line. Note that all hook and loop cable stays are not created equal. I have picked up bundles of hook and loop type cable stays over the years only to find out that they are cheap and not very good at their task. When you find a supplier, buy a small number of cable stays and see if they work strongly. You will know immediately if it is a good product once you get used to ones that in fact, are.

The proper method for rolling cable is known as over, under. You may have heard this term in the past but may not understand the method and concept of why it is important. Telling someone how to roll a cable over, under, is a hard task. It's a skill that is best learned by watching someone demonstrate the method in slow motion. A search of YouTube will give you an assortment of how-to videos.

* * *

Rolling your cables by this method will greatly extend their lifespan. The reason this is so is that as the cable is rolled in this way, the internal wires are not being forced to continually twist around each other. This method will produce a rolled cable, but the internal cables will virtually see their path as a straight line. If you continually roll the cable over-over, the cable will continually spin to the right internally causing damage over time. By rolling your cables with the over-under method, in a short amount of time you will have trained them to want to roll this way naturally. Teardown is greatly speeded up when your cables want to roll the correct way.

Time Alignment

Once you move beyond the simple left and right system and begin to add elements like separate subs or balcony speakers, time alignment of your components will become necessary. As the name implies, time alignment is simply the relationship between two speakers in space and time. Time alignment is measured in both feet and physical time. Sound will travel roughly at one foot every millisecond. Therefore the difference in time alignment between a mid/high box that is two feet behind a sub-cabinet in physical space is about 2 ms behind it in time. In this situation, the sub would need to be delayed about 2 ms, so when the original sound catches up to the sub 2 ms later, both sounds from both cabinets can then move on to the listener's ear in near perfect time alignment.

In professional sound, we use complex computer programs that have the ability to listen to and compare sound from multiple sources. We can observe sound impulses on a computer screen to see where the proper phase starts for any two sources. We can then use those time differences to delay certain parts of the system to bring the entire system into phase alignment. While highly accurate, most churches are not going to be able to afford this type of test gear. Nonetheless, time alignment is still something that needs to take place.

There are a few inferior methods that we use to get speakers time aligned into what I would refer to as a *ballpark area*. Without the aid of the computer and a program like Smaart, the next best substitute would be to take a measuring laser and measure the distance between the two points.

Let's look at a church building that has a left and right PA speaker by the stage and because of the length of the room, two more left and right speakers 40 feet back as delay speakers in the same room. If this sound system is not time aligned, listeners in the room are going to hear blurred sound coming from different points in the room at different times. We must delay the rear speakers by 40 feet to allow the sound from the front speakers to catch up to them. We would go into the send for those rear speakers on a processor or digital console and use a time delay setting to delay them 40 feet. This will be somewhere in the 40 ms range. Again, shooting a laser measure from the grill of the rear speaker to the grill of the front speaker will give you the rough distance in between the two.

Chapter 9

Biology & Acoustics

In order to understand the role acoustics play in how we perceive sound, we will need a short primer on how we perceive sound to begin with.

Transducers

Everything in sound engineering is a chain process. Everything, every sound, follows a path from its initial creation to its final destination, which is the brain of your audience. Along this journey, a sound will encounter a number of transducers. Simply put, a transducer is anything that transforms one type of energy into another.

Let's snap our fingers in a room, and follow this sound from its inception, to its final destination. When you snap your fingers, you cause pressure in your medium, and air molecules begin to crash into one another. This original energy is mechanical energy. This mechanical energy in the form of vibrations will move through the medium and will eventually encounter your microphone. The vibrations of the air molecules will apply pressure to the diaphragm in the mic and cause it to move in a sympathetic manner to the waves. At this point in the chain, the sound is still mechanical in nature.

At the microphone, the first transformation in the sound chain takes place. The mechanical movement of the diaphragm moves a coil of wire in and out of a magnetic field that will, in turn, produce a sympathetic electrical current corresponding to the waves. At this point, the mechanical energy has been transformed into electrical energy. The mic is the first transducer in this particular chain.

* * *

Once mechanical energy has been transformed into electrical energy, we are free to process it in any number of ways. We have electronic devices that can mix it with other electronic signals, alter its frequency balance, and vary its amplitude.

Electrical energy by its very nature is subject to degradation. Each time the electrical signal passes from one electrical circuit to another, a little bit of that signal is lost or altered. This is why on analog consoles you would see things like bypass switches on the EQ section. In modern consoles, we quickly transform this analog electrical energy into a digital code. We then keep the signal in this environment of information rather than electrical impulse for as long as possible. This handling of the signal is far superior because of the lack of normal signal degradation that naturally occurs in the analog environment.

At this stage, I should point out that we are still dealing with an electrical signal. We are simply talking about an improved method of handling that signal. Our reproduced sound will still suffer degradation similar to its analog counterpart, but the method of preservation throughout the stages of manipulation is superior. Let me put it this way, digital audio has done for sound reinforcement what refrigeration did for the food industry. It's all about preservation.

The Ear and the Body
Our bodies have been designed to be transducers of sound. We were designed from the very beginning of time to perceive and process sound. Our bodies take mechanical energy and transduce those impulses into bio-mechanical impulses that our brains can perceive and experience as sound.

The verbiage that I used in the previous paragraph may have stood out to you. A common misconception many people have is that we hear sound through our ears only. Our ears actually play but one part in our perception of sound. In a way, our multi-amped sound systems are merely crude mimics of how our bodies are designed to handle the various frequency ranges that we perceive.

Mid and high-frequency sounds do enter our bodies through the ears, but our bodies are also designed to use other parts to perceive different frequencies. Low midrange, for instance, enters into our bodies through our skulls. This is why your voice will sound different to you when you hear yourself on a recording. When you're listening to a recording, you will lack the frequencies that you would otherwise perceive from the vibrations in your skull as you talk. This is why a traffic director on a runway at an airport will wear hearing protection in the form of a headset rather than earplugs, which covers those bones on the side of the skull.

The lowest of frequencies are actually picked up by the rib cage. These low frequencies are then transmitted to the brain and added with the signals from all three locations and then mixed back into a composite signal in the brain. This is why people we refer to as deaf, can dance. Even a person who is totally deaf, can still hear at the lowest tones and feel the beat of the music. It is also why there is a low-frequency tone embedded in common sirens for ambulances and other emergency vehicles.

The ear itself processes those low mid to high frequencies by picking up sound in a similar fashion to a microphone. The eardrum can be likened to the diaphragm in a mic. Vibrations are transferred to a snail-shaped organ called the cochlea by way of three tiny bones which are in fact, the smallest bones in your body. The cochlea contains tiny hair-like receptors that respond to various frequencies from low to high, similar to keys on a piano. These impulses are then sent to the brain via auditory nerves.

The Brain
Now we really start to get into the Designer's programming. Once you start to understand the mathematical calculations that are going on in the human brain when it comes to the perception of sound, you will really begin to appreciate the complex programming that went into this ability that we take for granted on a daily basis.

The more you look at the algorithms that are needed and the precise complex computerized execution that is needed to perceive sound, the more you will realize that this is not a product of random chance or selective evolution. It is a masterfully crafted, mathematical program, designed and executed by a superior engineer. It is the ultimate beautiful coding of a master programmer.

The brain takes in all of these impulses from all of these mechanical sources and combines them into a solitary signal that a body can understand as sound, but that's not enough. The body must be able to place these sounds in a physical time and space to be able to perceive them as a three-dimensional landscape in order to actually know where a sound is coming from.

Enter stereophonic hearing. The brain accomplishes this by using two sound receptors instead of one. These two receptors are spaced out on your head about six or seven inches apart. This distance differs from person to person and each individual brain must compensate for these distances with its own individual unique algorithms.

These two receptors hear the same sound that is generated in an acoustical space and transmit those two distinct signals to the brain at relatively the same time. The brain uses those two signals obtained at slightly different intervals (remember those ears are six inches or so apart) and it extrapolates the time differences between the two sources to map a location for the original signal that it is hearing. That extrapolation is analyzed by the brain and a location is derived from the time differences that the data has provided. This process is going on an innumerable amount of times every second of every day, providing the brain with the data it needs to do its computations. Evolution and random chance or intelligent programming?

To understand sound at this level of design and attribute it to random chance, is in my opinion, insulting. I have genuine pity for any intelligent, educated engineer who fully understands the physics of sound and the biology of it, who writes it off as random chance and then finds himself one day standing before the programmer of this infinitely complex mathematical process and shrugs.

Sound Does Not Travel *Line of Sight*
Now we will begin to look at how the acoustics of the space in which we are mixing affects the sound that is traveling through the medium of that space. They are generally spherical in nature. When a sound occurs, it will not beam out in a straight line but rather emanates in multiple directions from its initial source. Higher frequencies will tend to be more directional, with lower frequencies being more omnidirectional.

The sounds emanate out and encounter the various surfaces within that space. The makeup of the surfaces will dictate the properties and qualities of what we commonly referred to as the acoustics. All surfaces will have a degree of reflectivity and absorption qualities that will affect sound at different frequencies. A certain wall or material in a room may absorb sound at certain frequencies and may reflect sound at others.

Direct and Reflected Sound
As your sound travels out into the room in a myriad of directions, some sounds will find their way directly to each ear in the listening space. Others will find their way to walls and other reflective surfaces. When the signals find those surfaces they will either be absorbed or reflected. Reflections are seldom total, but rather selected frequencies are reflected back into the acoustical space according to the properties of the reflective surface.

Here is where it starts to get crazy. As these direct and reflected sounds make their way to your ears, an internal process begins to make sense of it all. The more reverberant a room, the harder time the brain will have discerning between all of those signals with which it is being bombarded. An engineer will fatigue faster in a more reverberant room compared to an outdoor open space.

* * *

Let's look at an example of this in action. Let's say a simple sound starts in a room and makes its way directly to both of your ears. It has arrived at both of your ears somewhere between a theoretical zero and at a six-inch difference in time and space. Now at the same time, for simplicity sake, let's say that that sound has also bounced off of one hundred objects in the room and has arrived at both of your ears, each signal being between a theoretical zero and six inches apart in space and time.

Your brain, in real-time, takes in all of these signals and processes them to locate the most direct usable signal it can find. At the same time, it analyzes the other sounds in the room that would mask or smear the original and calculates which one is the most intelligible and literally rejects the rest. This process is going on every second of every day in your head.

In the heads of non-sound engineers this process is going on continually and the person is never aware of it. A sound engineer, however, is keenly aware of it and in time will train himself to notice the reflections that others simply cannot hear, or more accurately, do not notice.

As an exorcise you might want to try sitting in the center of a room with a partner. Take turns talking to each other one at a time. As your partner is talking, try to get your brain to zone out on your partners original direct sound and try to listen instead to the four walls in the building, concentrating on one at a time. In time, with training, you will begin to be able to actually hear the walls as your brain is retrained to critically listen for them.

An easy way to jump-start this process is to defeat the system. Yes, this is cheating, but it will help you in your critical listening development by showing you what you're actually listening for. As we stated before, the brain uses that space between your ears to extrapolate time differentials. You can defeat the process to some degree by taking one of your two ears out of the equation. Perform the same exercise as you did above but this time take your little finger and seal off one of your ears as best as you can. This will take the majority of the data received from that receptor out of the mathematical equation process in the brain. The results will be that the brain can no longer efficiently determined directionality. Once directionality is taken out of the mathematical equation, it will no longer have that data to process and determine which sounds it should reject. You will then begin to hear the sound that your brain is actually rejecting.

Again, attributing this level of computation and programming to chance is simply ludicrous. It would be like accepting that my new drone had figured out the ability to fly out to a random place in time and return precisely on its own without any outside programming. And then after it figured it out, it gained the ability somehow to do it perfectly every time from that point on.

Chapter 10

Reverberation

In this chapter we will again look at acoustics, but this time from the vantage point of reverberation time. We will explore how these properties affect our mix, and we will learn the skills needed to understand reflections and room properties.

Acoustics is a science unto itself. I am a live sound engineer and wish to point out that I do not consider myself an acoustician. As such this chapter is only going to tackle reverberation and room acoustics from the vantage point of the live sound engineer. We will be going over some of the basic things that you will deal with when you're behind the console.

Live, Dead, and Musical
Even if you're mixing outdoors, there is always something for sound to reflect off of. Indoors you will have many reflective surfaces, and as such, many reflections that you will deal with as a sound engineer. Buildings designed to be listening spaces, such as churches, will almost always have to be designed in such a way that reflections are minimized.

When we do large installations, we will work with acousticians to tune the room even as we tune the PA. The two most common treatments in buildings are absorption and diffusion. Absorption is accomplished using panels and building materials that absorb sound and do not allow certain frequencies to reflect. Diffusion controls sound by bouncing sound into a different direction than it was originally traveling in when it strikes the surface. Diffusion can be in the form of half tube-shaped objects in a room which are designed to scatter the sound. Every wall, every seat, and every surface, like a floor or ceiling, are reflective surfaces. As stated in the previous chapter our brains will tend to tune out the majority of these reflections in order for sound to be intelligible to our brains.

Interestingly enough, the brain will not tune out these reflections in totality. It will retain a small amount of these reflections in order to enhance sound on an artistic level. It will allow enough reflections through as to enhance the quality and timbre of tones. Because your brain does not tune out 100% of the reflected matter, spaces will all sound different.

We refer to spaces in three different acoustical ways. We will refer to them as live, dead, or musical. A live space is a space with a high reverberation time or what we refer to as *R factor*. The R factor of a room is measured with a complex formula developed by Wallace Sabine in the late 1800s. What we call the RT60 method of R factor determination is still the standard today. Though the RT60 formula is a complex mathematical equation that takes in many variables, for your purpose behind a console, the only thing you really need to know is that the R factor of a space is simply the time a sound takes to decay 60 dB from its original start (or simply the time that it takes for it to become inaudible to the human ear) and is measured in seconds.

For our purposes, we can get a quick idea of the R time in a given space by doing a crude unscientific test of the space with testing devices that we all carry, our hands and ears. You can get a quick down and dirty idea of where a room is acoustically, or at least as far as how intelligible it might be, by simply walking into a quiet room and clapping. On the initial clap, count off seconds with the one one-thousand, two one-thousand, three one-thousand method until you can no longer hear the decay of the hand clap.

If you cannot hear any decay, you are standing in what we would call an acoustically dead room. An acoustically dead room will sound dry and as the name implies, musically dead. The engineer will typically have to artificially add reverb to key elements of the mix to get a pleasing musical environment.

* * *

If you are able to make it to two seconds, you are in an acoustically live space. A higher degree of engineering skill will be required, and your mix will not be as good as it would be in a musical space. You'll also be limited to the amount of artificial reverberation that can be added to the mix because of the natural reverberation that is already present. Adding more reverb in a room like this will just continue to muddy the sound even further.

If you can count to three seconds in a given space, know that you are in an inhospitable environment for engineering sound. While you may be able to take some measures to get by, your job in this space is going to be one of survival, not art.

If your claps are falling in the one second to one and a half second range, you are in the Goldilocks zone, not too dead, not to live, and hopefully musical. Why do I say hopefully? Because reverb time is not the only factor in a musical room. The R factor only tells us how fast general sound is dissipating in the space. You must remember that all frequencies decay at different rates in different spaces. But by following this general rule of thumb with this crude method of analyzing a room, you are going to have a good idea, even before you plug in the sound system whether or not a room is going to sound good. In time with experience and practice, you will be able to determine the R factor of a room with relative accuracy by simply walking into the room and listening to a conversation.

Resonant Frequencies
The next thing we are going to look at in this chapter is the resonant frequency of a room. Every physical space will have a frequency to which that space is tuned. That is to say that every space will have a frequency at which it will resonate or vibrate.

When I was a kid we did not have plastic bottles for our sodas as we have today. In my day, every soda you would buy at the grocery store came either in a can or a glass bottle. As you drank your soda, you could blow across the top of your Coke bottle and hear a tone or pitch. As you drank more of your Coke, the pitch would lower. This is an example of the airspace within the enclosure resonating. In the case of this example, the enclosure is the Coke bottle.

Speaker manufacturers understand this principle and employ it when tuning cabinets for better low-frequency reproduction. Those holes and slots in speaker cabinets are there for a reason. They tune the resonant frequency of that cabinet to a specific frequency that would be difficult for the speaker to reproduce on its own. In effect, it uses the physics of resonance to emphasize a frequency that would otherwise be lost. It is not uncommon for a speaker cabinet to be tuned to fifty or sixty hertz. The loudspeaker on its own would have a difficult time reproducing that sound, however with the proper porting, or tuning, we can cause the cabinet to resonate at that frequency and reproduce it by means of resonance.

Think of the room in which you are mixing as a large speaker enclosure. It shares the same characteristics as a bass cabinet. It is simply a larger space. Like the speaker enclosure, it is somewhat sealed. This space will also have a frequency at which it resonates. The majority of rooms are going to resonate somewhere in between 40 Hz and 300 Hz with the vast majority falling in between the 100 Hz and 200 Hz range.

Knowing the resident frequency of the room in which you are mixing sound is paramount to getting a good mix. Because the room is extra live at this particular frequency, it will tend to become an area of your mix that is problematic. The resonant frequency of the room will also affect all other low-frequency properties of what you're mixing by way of harmonics. In other words, if you have a room with a resonant frequency of 120 Hz, you will also see a slight increase at 240 Hz. In fact, you will often find if you are having issues with a certain frequency in a room, let's say at 400 Hz, you can often times trace that causality back to the resonant frequency of the room at 200 Hz.

* * *

The resonant frequency of a room can be determined by listening to the low-frequency portion of your mix. There will be an area of your mix that will *bump* or standout compared to adjacent frequencies. This can be determined in a few different ways. You can play recorded music in the room and listen to how the low end is responding. If you take the low-frequency gain on your channel strip for your music playback and raise it say 3 or 6 dB and then sweep the frequency on the EQ section, there will be a place that seems to do more than any other spot in the frequency range. That is usually the resonant frequency in the room. You can also visually see a resonant frequency of a room by running pink noise in a room and observing a real-time analyzer, or RTA. There will be a slight bump in the resonant frequency range of around 3 to 6 dB.

If you attend a concert in an arena and are able to see the engineers house graphic EQ, you will almost always see a slight dip somewhere in the sub 400 Hz range. This is compensating for the resonant frequency of the room. You will also likely have an area dipped on your own church EQ somewhere between 100 and 300 Hz. Go take a look. If your system is properly tuned to your room, you've probably already found the resonant frequency without even knowing that you did.

Standing Waves
A standing wave occurs when you have two parallel surfaces in a room that will allow a sound to bounce back and forth between them. This can be any parallel surface. It could be one wall facing another. It could be the surface between a stage wall and a balcony front. While we're at it, let's remember that sound is three dimensional. Let's not just think of X and Y but also Z. It can also be the sound reflected from the ceiling to the floor.

To better understand the standing wave phenomenon, let's think about something that we can see. Let's compare it to playing pool. When you hit a pool ball on the pool table it will reflect off a bumper. If there is no spin on the ball it will reflect off the bumper in the opposite angle that it hits. Sound behaves in precisely the same way. This is why the actual placement of your speakers in a room is critical to controlling standing waves. With a small portable PA system, you can improve the acoustics of the room by simply tilting your speakers slightly inward instead of facing them directly at the back wall. This will cause the sound to hit the back wall at a slight angle. Remember our pool table? This will cause the sound to deflect instead of reflect. Just remember that on the pool table you are only dealing with X and Y. In the real world of sound, you're dealing with X, Y, and Z.

When we engineer a permanent sound system to a room, whether it be a line array system or a column array system, we are choosing boxes and patterns that will minimize the amount of sound that reflects directly off of hard surfaces such as the side and back walls. We are also trying to minimize sound that would go upward into the ceiling or roll back onto the stage.

Old as Dirt
Modern-day acoustic treatment really became prevalent in the 40s and 50s. Post World War II era schools commonly used sound panels throughout their construction to help with the acoustics. Through the 60s and 70s these panels became prevalent in churches and government buildings as well. Through the 70s and 80s we learned more and more about how to build panels to defuse and absorb sound. In the two-thousands we have reached a state-of-the-art in the design and construction of buildings in regards to acoustics.

As a sound engineer, I am amused when I read my Bible and take note that God was fully aware of what we would refer to as modern acoustic treatments 3000 years ago. You don't have to look any further than one of the largest building projects recorded in the Bible, that of King Solomon's Temple. The Bible actually lays out a blueprint for the two main rooms of the temple, one being the holy of holies and the other the holy place. The holy place was a rectangular room made of stone. The holy of holies was also made of stone, but it was a perfect cube.

Three thousand years later with modern technology and computer modeling, we can precisely know what the acoustics would've been in that temple, and they would not have been good. When those rooms were finished, they were finished with what we would consider modern state-of-the-art diffusion and absorption techniques. Fir was used for absorption in the rooms and the walls were lined with evenly spaced sculptures that defused the sound at regular intervals. It's taken us three-thousand years, but we have finally caught up to God's construction techniques.

Chapter 11

If Bad Sound Were Toxic, We'd All Be Dead

It's true. Bad sound is all around us. As a professional engineer, I cannot go to someone else's show and not pick apart the sound. That is the curse of doing this for a living. But sometimes we can be better at something simply by learning what is good, by observing what is bad. In this chapter we are going to take a look at some of the more prevalent ways in which good sound goes south so we might be better equipped to understand what to do *right*.

The Pareto Principle
The other day I sat in my Chiropractor's office chatting with him. In our conversation I posed the question; "Gary, In my profession, there are probably 20% of us that are considered world class. About 30% of us are what we would refer to as hacks, the majority take up the remaining average. What do you suppose the ratio is in your field?"

Gary responded, "Oh you're referring to the 80/20 rule. I would say it's pretty much the same in my profession, and if the 80/20 rule holds true, it can be said for almost anything in life."

The 80/20 rule was conceived by Vilfredo Pareto in the late 1800s. The premise was dictated by his observation that people in society seem to divide naturally into what he called, *the vital few* or, the top 20% in terms of influence, power, intelligence, and money making in whatever areas in which they were involved. In other words, the top 20% ruled the world, or at least influenced their corner of it, and the remaining 80% simply followed along.

Now I consider Gary to be in the top 20% in his field, and he considers me to be in the top of mine. This entire book takes the approach of teaching from that top 20 percent, but I think it might be fun to swim in the shallow end of the sound reinforcement pool for a while. There is much to be learned by looking at how to do it wrong, and according to Pareto, there is a lot more data on that end of the spectrum than at the top. Because of this, I'll apologize right now, because this will, undoubtably, be the longest chapter in the book.

When you Break Rules, There are Consequences

Sound reinforcement in one respect, is a game. You are manipulating the physical properties of the world around you. This game has rules. They are the rules of science and design. As with any game, if you master the rules, and understand them, you will have success in what you do. Conversely, if you ignore those rules, or do not properly understand them, you will pay the consequences when those rules are broken. If you are a person who wants to fight the rules, change the rules, bend the rules, or make up your own, you will experience grief.

Poor Acoustics

The first area I'll start off with, ironically, has little to do with sound engineers. It has to do with ignorance and a lack of planning on the part of builders. The acoustic design of a church facility will be the largest contributing factor to how well a system will be able to do its job.

As a professional installer, we typically see two approaches when it comes to church building design. In the first instance, we will come in alongside the builder at ground level and work with an acoustician to design the space to be musical. This method is the most cost-effective and yields the best results.

In the second method, a church or builder will simply construct a box in the most cost-effective way possible, leaving acoustics to be dealt with at a later time, and usually at someone else's expense. This second method is by far the most costly way of dealing with the key element which is in fact, the primary function of your space, the engineered ability to be heard and understood.

The reason for this is simple but commonly ignored. We're going to look at an example and use a point system instead of monetary values to drive home a point. After all, the budgets will change in proportion to the size of the project, but the end results will be the same.

If you have a building project and dedicate a budget of 10 on a scale of 1-10 for acoustics, you will get 100% out of your PA. If you save 8 initially and spend 2 on the same project, you will get 20% out of your PA that you spent 100% on. You will then back peddle into survival mode and spend 20 on your 1-10 scale in order to get to an acceptable 50% of your PA. This demonstrates the vital importance of budgeting for acoustics in the initial phase of building

Learning the Limits of Our System and Our Ears
There are fewer places that I routinely see the rules being broken, then in the area of exceeding limits. I don't care if you're sitting in church or going to a large show at a 10,000 seat arena. If you walk out of that event and your ears hurt, you have been subject to an engineer who does not understand limits.

While exceeding the limit of the human ear may not be deadly in and of itself, it can certainly be damaging, and that damage may well be permanent. As a sound engineer, we have been charged with control over an art form that can actually be a sort of unintentional weapon. That is to say that it can inflict injury, and as such, the person wielding this power must fully understand limits. This is a huge responsibility and should be respected as such.

After four decades of engineering sound, I can put up a mix without the aid of a dB meter present and know exactly where my RMS (Root Mean Square) level is in the room within about one dB. Even though I have this experience, I routinely keep a dB meter off to my side running pretty much throughout the entirety of any show I am engineering.

***

Having a meter by your side as you are mixing is not enough. You must also have a good working knowledge of what that information is telling you. My primary reasons for monitoring the dB meter are two-fold. Number one, it will tell me how loud instantaneous peaks might have been as they go by. This way I will know what my absolute peak was during a mixing session. It will also confirm that my ears are not fatiguing. It is a visual reference and means of comparing what my brain is thinking, what my ears are hearing, and the actual reality of what is taking place in the room. When I put all three of these elements together, I will know exactly where I am at any given moment as an engineer.

Fatigue

We all understand that athletes need to be physically fit, and if you are going to participate in any athletic endeavor, you are going to have a training regiment to keep your body fit. You will understand that over time you will get better and better at what you're setting out to do as your body responds to the training that you are giving it.

Athletes understand the concept of peaking. They understand that there will be a sweet spot in their performance curve where they will be at their utmost ability to perform their task at hand, whether it be a sprint, a jump, or a run. Long distance runners pace themselves. They know that there will be a time for which they must save their peak performance, and they know their body is not capable of performing within that peak zone for more than a set amount of time.

You may not currently be aware of it, but the same principles apply to sound reinforcement and sound engineering. When we first start running sound our ears will have a very small window of peak performance. Our brains will also have a very small window of attention span when it comes to critical listening. When we first start engineering sound our ears may only be able to work at peak efficiency for a half an hour before they begin to fatigue.

* * *

When I was a young engineer I would spend hours and hours mixing street fairs and festivals. This was incredible training and it served me well as an engineer later in life. Ear fatigue and the ability to critically listen for long periods of time is a skill that you may develop through practice and training. It's like a workout regimen of lifting weights. You can think of it as weight training for your brain.

You may not have the opportunity to go out and work street fairs with eight-hour mixing sessions, but you do need to be aware that this is a skill that you will develop over time, and you will develop it simply by doing. The longer you mix sound, the better your body will get at pushing off that fatigue over longer and longer periods of time.

If you're reading this book and you are not a sound engineer but someone on the worship team, a pastor, or a congregant, at some point you may have a time where you hear something going on in your room and you glance back at your sound engineer and wonder why isn't he hearing that? Why isn't he fixing that? The simple answer to the question, especially if he is a young engineer, is that it could be that he no longer *does* hear it. This can be a new concept for people to understand, but for everyone no matter who you are, there is a point where the brain simply tunes out.

In the engineer's defense, the answer may be more complex. He may actually be in the process of curing it, but he may be dealing with the problem slower than you think it should be dealt with, or he might have prioritized another issue first. Backseat engineering is an easy task when you only have one thing on your mind that is bothering you. Remember your sound engineer is juggling a myriad of things at once.

Time and training is the only thing that will stretch your peak performance level. So what can you do if you find yourself fatiguing on a given day? Sometimes simply walking away and taking a break will snap your brain back into its proper place of attention. In the middle of a service may not be the most opportune time for you to do that, and that's understandable. During those times if you feel yourself drifting off, know that that is probably the time you should start trying harder to pay attention. This is where the heavy lifting comes in, and in time you will begin to stretch that attention span.

Boosting Instead of Cutting

One of the most common amateur engineering mistakes I routinely see sound people make is finding the frequency that is the most annoying in a mix and boosting it. This happens when a soundman is mixing from a place of cause and reaction instead of analyzation and action. Psychologically, the soundman is simply listening for something to happen. By boosting a frequency that is already too hot, it causes a very apparent change in sound. Unfortunately, this is not a change for the better.

If you're reading this and wondering, oh my, am I that guy? Do some research in your own mix. Try going to your vocal channels. Look at your EQ section on those channels. Are you boosting in the 300 to 800 Hz region? This range typically has the most unwanted frequencies where vocal mics are concerned. If you see boosts on your EQ at these points, you may be guilty.

Another place to look is on the kick drum channel. Is there boosting going on in the 200 to 400 Hz region? Kick drums normally have an abundance of these frequencies in the shells and they routinely need to be cut out. If there's boosting going on in these frequencies, you know you have a problem. It could be a horrible kick drum in need of replacement, it could be a horrible microphone, or the problem just might be with ...dare I say....the engineer.

Oversaturation

Over saturation is the most common place where I see mistakes being made on a professional level. We see it with engineers who have not yet mastered the concept that everything has limits and everything has a saturation point. I have brought this point out numerous times in this book, and it's bound to come up numerous times again. The stubborn blatant reality is if you oversaturate a room or any piece of gear, you will damage your mix. The heavier the over-saturation, the worse a mix will become. The longer you oversaturate your ears and the ears of your audience, the more that fatigue will set in.

Gain Structure
Here's a common telephone call I take on a semi-regular basis. "Hey, we're having a problem at our church. We can't seem to get our monitors loud enough on stage. All of our monitor mixes are turned up almost all the way, and we still can't get enough gain. What's wrong?"

The question may take a lot of different forms, but usually, the answer is the same. Sometimes the church won't be able to get enough signal to the device that is recording the services. Other times they may not have enough gain into an auxiliary mix like a cry room. The problem could be anywhere in the system, but the problem is usually the same regardless of its location. The problem is usually gain structure or more accurately, improper gain structure.

I've gone out to many a church to do a service call for these types of issues. A very common place for the entire problem to start, whatever it may be, is at the very beginning. A church that does not understand gain structure usually does not understand what the gain knob does on the input of every channel of their console. The fact is, if you don't get a gain structure set up correctly on the head amp of your console from the very beginning, you will stand a very slim chance of getting proper gain structure set throughout the rest of your entire system. In other words, you have to start off on the right foot to begin with instead of trying to make up for it later on down the road.

Drowning in the Mix
Reverb usage is another place where you see abuse happening in a mix. Properly applied reverb can be the icing on the cake, an

enhancement that makes a good mix sound great. You can also have the unintentional result of drowning in a mix. We've all heard vocalist going down in the deep end of the pool without a life preserver. Common mistakes here include putting reverb on too many things in the mix, using too much reverb, and using too long of a reverb. Too much of a good thing is no longer a good thing.

Noise

Noise can be defined as any unwanted sound in your mix. Noise is to sound as weeds are to a flower garden. Noise can come from a lot of different places, but one of the most common causes of electronic noise in the mix is a buzzing amplifier.

As the sound engineer, you are the last stop for noise in the sound chain. Think of yourself as the noise police. It never ceases to amaze me that certain guitarists or bass players are perfectly fine with their rig buzzing at a volume that is nearly as loud as they are playing. Often times when pointed out they'll say, "Oh, yes, I hear that now that you point it out." More often than not, it will be your job to figure out why an instrument is buzzing and what to do to get rid of it.

Another common introduction of noise into the mix is caused by bad gain structure. If your gain is turned down too far and you're trying to make up for it in other places, you're going to be raising your noise floor along with your sound. Pay attention to gain structure!

The Phantom Instrument

It's so annoying when you go to a show and there is a specific instrument onstage that you cannot hear at all. This one is probably harder for us to take as sound engineers because we have to sit in the audience knowing there's nothing we can personally do about it. The best revenge that you could have when it comes to this mixing faux pas is; *don't be that guy*. Once you have your mix sounding great, sit back and listen to it as a whole.

* * *

As engineers we must to switch to a different mode in our brains. We have to focus on individual instruments during sound check, but when we begin to actually mix, we need to switch gears back to listening to the mix as a whole entity. Imagine that you are listening to an album at home. Can you hear everything in your mix? Is everything balanced as it needs to be? When you're at someone else's show, as you see the phantom instrument playing on stage, you can be sure that you are listening to an engineer who has not mastered that switch mode in his brain.

Inability to Hear
It is not uncommon in my job to find myself dealing with a professional engineer who is in effect, deaf. It happens a lot more than you might think. The vast majority of deaf people are not what we would refer to as *totally deaf*. A totally deaf person would be an individual who has lost most of their hearing in the frequency range above 400 Hz. Even a totally deaf person is still going to be able to feel the lowest of low frequencies. So when I referred to a deaf person, I refer to any person who is deaf in a specific frequency range, most commonly high frequencies.

As we age we will lose more and more of our high-frequency hearing range. It is inevitable, and it is part of the aging process. Over time with continuous exposure to sound pressure, the small hairs in the internal ear begin to bend over and do not recover. The flatter these nerve endings become, the less of those frequencies we will be able to hear.

As I am writing this book I am approaching my sixties. I am keenly aware of the hearing loss that has occurred with my ears throughout my lifetime. Throughout my career, I've continually checked my ears with tone generators in order to know exactly where I am and to be able to track my loss as I age. At my age, I am well past that sweet spot of a touring sound engineer. My only defense in this aging process is my experience that tells me what I can no longer hear.

* * *

If a person does not understand this process and is not keenly aware of the natural loss that happens over time, they will begin to compensate by turning up what they can no longer hear. This is usually what is happening when you go to a show and you see someone in their fifties or sixties mixing, and you feel like your head is about to be taken off with a hi-hat.

At my stage of life, I fully realize that my prime mixing era has passed. It does not keep me from spending time behind the sound console, but it does limit what I can effectively do now. When I was in my thirties and forties, I had a reputation as a high fidelity sound engineer. In my sixties, you may find me behind a console at a church event or corporate event, but it would be unlikely to find me behind the console of a nationally touring high fidelity band. Knowing your physical abilities and limitations at all stages of life is critical in sound reinforcement.

While we're on the subject, this is probably a good time to talk about how critical it is to protect your own ears. Any time you are in an environment that makes your ears ring, you are damaging your ears. Now, that damage can be temporary or permanent. Hearing protection is critical in any and all situations where loud noises are present.

Common power tools, gardening tools like leaf blowers, and similar items can all cause permanent hearing loss. Always wear hearing protection sufficient for whatever task you're doing, or whatever environment you're in. If you're not getting ribbed every now and then for being ridiculous with your use of hearing protection, you're probably going to pay the price later on in life. You are a soundman, you should know better than the common man on the street or your friends. Wear appropriate protection!

Wind
There are things I love about mixing outdoors, and there are things I hate. The wind would be in the hate category. There are few things more challenging than getting a lectern mic hot enough

on a pulpit, with a quiet speaker, on a day with 30 mph wind. Your defense here is to remove as much of the wind noise as possible.

Running sound is often likened unto a surgical procedure. We say that we are EQ'ing with surgical precision. We cut and remove portions of the sound that are unwanted, etc. This being the case, we can look at mixing in wind as amputation. Yes, I can take the cancer out of the mix, but the leg comes with it.

Successfully mixing in the wind requires you to leave as many microphones closed (muted) onstage as possible, and as for the ones that are open, you must hi pass the channels until the wind has been minimized to a point that is bearable. As you do this, the low-frequency body and the fidelity of the sound is going to go with it. The trick is to leave enough to be tolerable while taking away the wind noise that is detrimental to the operation of the sound system.

In Tune
The musicians on stage being in tune is something that you have little control over as a sound engineer. No, sound consoles are not yet available with autotune on every channel. There are a few things that you can do to get by when tuning on stage is an issue.

If the problem is an instrument, have your musician tune their instrument during soundcheck. I know that sounds quite basic, but if it's that obvious, stop and have them tune. The problem may lie in a defective instrument that cannot be properly tuned. In that case, your only hope is to replace the instrument.

Vocals are a little more of a challenge. Generally speaking, you never want to be so callous as to walk up to a worship team member and tell them, "Wow, you can't sing, can you?" I have worked professionally with artists in national act that have continuous pitch problems that cannot be avoided; they simply have to be dealt with.

A background vocalist can be dealt with easier than a lead vocalist. Pitchy background vocals can simply be slightly lowered in the mix. In this circumstance, masking is your friend. Add a little reverb to blend that vocal in, and make sure the stronger vocal is on the top. You'll also find a pitchy vocalist will need just a little bit more monitor than a good vocalist to stay on pitch.

Talking in the Toilet

This one's a pet peeve of mine, the soundman that is just too lazy to mute the worship leaders reverb in between songs. You can go from angelic cathedral vocals to listening to a conversation in the men's restroom just that fast by leaving them in the tank in between songs.

If this is you, good news! You can be a noticeably better sound engineer by simply muting your vocal reverb in between songs. There is something psychological that will take place when you do. Your vocals will stand out more, and the important message between them will as well. It's a win, win, and the simplest 100% improvement in your sound that you can make. Give it a try; you'll go from amateur soundman to sounding more like a pro in a single Sunday.

Bad Drums

When it comes to your worship team, the drums are usually the foundation of your mix. It is typically the place where you start and then build the entire mix from there. When you're starting off with a bad drum kit, you are starting off with a bad foundation. You will find that a good drum kit, with properly live heads, are essential to getting a great worship team mix.

So many times I've had people come up to me at a professional show and compliment me on how well everything sounds coming through the sound system. I have heard comments like, "Man I wish I could get my PA to sound that good at my church." Though I'd like to take full credit for the great sound, there's actually a lot that must happen before I pull out my mics at the beginning of the day.

* * *

One simple factor is that on a professional show you are almost always starting off with professional sounding gear. It is highly unusual to show up for a professional show in an arena to see a road crew assembling a drum kit with worn-out heads.

While we're on the topic of drums, another faux pas is using microphones that are specifically tuned for drums on other instruments. The classic that I see all the time is a bass player using a Shure B52 to mic a bass cabinet instead of a bass drum. It's all bass, right? Wrong. A B52 has a radical frequency pattern that has been specifically designed to do one thing and one thing only, make a kick drum sound great. Placing this mic on a bass guitar will result in removing all of the tones that you want to be present in your bass and amplifying all the muddy lower overtones instead.

What Does the Square Speaker Do?

You see it all the time, something placed in front of a speaker cabinet. It might be a pillar, it might be a decretive plant or tree. The rule of thumb here folks is, if you can't look down the throat of a horn, you can't hear it either.

You would think that musicians would be the most knowledgable next to the soundman when it comes to this concept, but alas, they are often the worse offenders. I've seen monitors trying to shoot through keyboards, music stands, and piano benches. I've even seen horns taped over with set lists. I've seen monitors pointing at every part of the body except the part you hear with.

The second most common mistake made is tilting a box on its side, defeating the horns acoustical pattern in the process. Now there are times when I might put a fifteen horn box on its side to purposefully tighten its horn pattern, such as when I'm using it as a drum wedge, but generally, you're using physics to shoot your sound in the foot if you're doing this with a house PA box.

Death Rains Down From Above

I was working on an installation once in San Francisco in a concrete building. Another install company had installed a PA system in a corporate boardroom with hanging pendant speakers. The company was an electrical company and not a specialized sound company, such as ours, needed for this type of installation. We were brought in after the original installation was found to be problematic. Actually, that's a nice way of saying it just didn't work.

Upon our initial inspection, we found a rack stuffed into a corner cupboard that had a cluster of boxes and cables that loosely resembled some type of small rodents nest. The original install was so shoddy that we simply had no other choice than to hand grenade it and basically start over from scratch.

The big surprise came when I climbed the ladder in the boardroom to inspect the many hanging pendant speakers that hung directly over all the board members heads. When I simply touched the first speakers rigging cable the entire speaker assembly pulled out of the ceiling and fell to the floor, being stopped only by the tie straps that held its speaker cables in place. Upon closer examination, it was discovered that the original speakers were suspended from the concrete by means of a Hilti nail gun. Nails where used instead of anchors and they simply went into the concrete at a depth of about an eighth of an inch.

Any installer worth his salt knows that San Francisco has a way of testing the ruggedness of everything in a structural build. The city will shake every few years, so you had better know what you're doing any time you fly something over people's heads. In this instance, bad sound could have been deadly.

Your church may be far from San Francisco, but when it comes to rigging, the same rules apply. If you're going to fly, leave the fly up to professionals who know what they're doing. The safety of your congregation depends upon it. You cannot fly overhead items by chains, turnbuckles, and quick links bought at the local hardware store. Flying heavy items in a sound, light, or video rig requires specialized knowledge and specialized fly rated hardware. Please don't be tempted to save a buck here. Hire a professional to do the job right. Lives literally depend on it.

Shocking!

While we're on the topic of how to kill someone, it's important to note a common mistake that is often times fatal. If you do a Google search for baptism death, you'll get a string of results. A surprising number of people over the years have gone home to be with the Lord during their baptism.

The common cause of most of these deaths can be attributed to people climbing into baptismal water while the officiant is holding onto a wired microphone. The key factor here is the phrase *wired*. A wired microphone can create a path to live voltage looking for a better way to ground via a larger conductor. A pool of water is a very large conductive body, and a human body is the perfect path to complete that circuit. The end result is a baptism that never makes it past the *dead in sin* phase. I read about one pastor who's prayer of "Lord, surprise me!" was immediately answered as he stepped into the water. That's not a joke, by the way; it actually happened.

You may think that placing the mic on a stand in front of the baptismal is a good idea. It is not in your hand and you don't plan on touching it. Sounds like it will work out well. The problem here is that I can't tell you how many failing mic clips I've seen over the years. If that mic clip decides to suddenly flop forward, you're toast.

What about using a wireless mic then? While the risk of death generally transfers from the people in the tank to the mic itself, I have to strongly admonish everyone, electronics and water don't mix! Don't do it! Keep all of your electronics out of the baptismal area. Conduct any interviews, and wrap up your introductions before the actual baptism commences, then climb into the water completely free of anything electronic.

* * *

The Cable Roll
In California, we love our sushi. I'm always amused at the many different names chefs come up with for their rolls. We're kind of the same way with sound. As we touched on previously, improperly wound cable is not only frustrating but can lead to the cables' demise. In this section, we'll look at a few of the classic cable roll blunders.

At the top of the list, we must start with the classic *Elbow Roll*. In this classic technique, the cable (regardless of type) is rolled tightly by wrapping it around the hand and elbow. Nothing say's *I have no idea what I'm doing* quite like the elbow roll. This method will eventually break down the cable internally as the cable itself will twist continually as it is wrapped. This method will also produce the frustrating yet decorative figure 8 design.

The next roll is the classic *Professional Contractor Roll*. When you see this person rolling one of your power cords in the classic construction worker fashion, you might feel like walking over and saying, "Need a hard hat?" But don't. These people are usually professionals, just not in your particular field. As such, they are often open to learning the tricks of other trades. They also usually have an appreciation for the other trades. More often than not, they can be quite teachable.

Worse yet is the *No Roll*. This is the *wad it up and throw it in a box* method of cable storage. Take time and effort to learn how to roll and store your cables. Again, take good care of them, and they will take good care of you.

* * *

The Shy or Inconsistent Vocalist

Thank God for the invention of the radio. The invention of the radio led to the invention of the audio compressor. Early compressors were used to avoid over-modulation of the audio signal. Today it is one of the few tools in our toolbox that will help address the shy or inconsistent vocalist.

If you mix sound, you will inevitably deal with this person. The singer that continually asks you to turn up their monitor. Typically you will walk up to their wedge, speak loudly into their vocal mic, and blow yourself into the back of the stage.

What's going on here is simple physics. You cannot amplify something that is not there. If the singer is not confident, they will typically sing quietly. I have had vocalists that talk in between songs at twice the volume at which they sing.

This is not a professional singer. A confident singer, sings, but guess what? Our churches do not typically have professional singers, we have volunteers. In reality, there is little you can do to get a shy person to sing louder, especially if they are compounding the problem by not singing into their mic. The only thing you can do generally is give them instruction on mic technique, and add compression to their channel to bring down the peaks they hit so that they will be at the same level as if they are whispering, and then try to amplify the whole signal as loud as you can before feedback.

With the shy vocalist, you also must be ready to simply say *no*. If you have that monitor as loud as you possibly can, and the request comes in again to be turned up, the answer is then, no. No is a legitimate answer in sound reinforcement. In fact, I try to treat my musicians the same way that I treated my daughter as I was raising her. I try to say yes whenever possible. Then in those times when I have to say no, they know that no means no. Will you be able to get an incredible sounding mix with professional sounding vocals with that shy vocalist? No.

Chapter 12

Mic Choice

In this chapter, we are going to look at the various mic choices that are out there and hopefully take any mystery or confusion out of the various types of mics available.

If I had a dime for every time I've walked into a church and seen a comical or curious mic choice, I'd be a rich man. Sometimes it's out of ignorance, while other times it is out of necessity. Sometimes it can even be downright dangerous! Did that grab your attention? OK, perhaps not dangerous to any person, but you can end the life of a mic simply by using it incorrectly. More on that to come.

There are a few different types of mics out there and it's important to understand that they all excel in certain areas. The flip side of the coin is that they will also be poor choices for other uses. There are very few examples of universal mics that work great on everything. The more educated you are on microphone types, the better you will be at choosing the sort that will work well for specific applications.

Some factors that will dictate your microphone choice are things like transient response and dynamic level. Transient response simply refers to how fast the microphone will respond when hit with a fast percussive signal like the hit of a drum head or the pluck of a string.

Dynamic level refers to how loud of a sound pressure level a microphone can take and reproduce before it overloads. You will want to choose a larger diaphragm microphone with the ability to take a larger sound pressure level for something like a kick drum as compared to a conga.

The Right Camera

Ask any professional photographer what the right camera is to take a specific picture, and they'll tell you that it's *the one that you have at the time*. That is to say, that even though specific mics might be most suited for specific things, the good engineer knows how to work with what's in his immediate arsenal to achieve his goals and meet his needs.

There are no absolute perfect mics for every situation. Much to do with mic choice is personal preference and availability. There are however two workhorses in the industry that have become the staple of any professional's work box. These two mics are relatively inexpensive, relatively flat in all the places they need to be, while offering slight boosts to the general overall sweet-spots in the audio spectrum that our ears generally find pleasing. They are readily available, and are as rugged as they come. Add all that up and it's easy to understand why the Shure SM58 vocal mic and Shure SM57 instrument mic have become the adopted world standard of generic go-to mics.

In any church installation that my company does that happens to need a complete complement of mics, they will get a fleet of 57s and 58s specced. Unless a specialty mic is needed, one of these mics is always a workable choice for a vocal or an instrument. Are these two always the best choice for mics? No, certainly not. If you are a vocalist, try a variety of mics. All vocal mics have differences, some subtle, some extreme, but if you're looking for the *works good on everything* vocal mic, grab a 58.

* * *

The DI

DI stands for *direct input*. It is more commonly called a direct box or DI for short. It will take a line or instrument level and convert it to a mic level signal that the board will see as a microphone at its input. Because of this, it will usually have a quarter inch input going into the box and an XLR output just like a microphone to plug into the sound system.

DIs can be active or passive. Active direct boxes have internal pre-amps that will need to be powered either off of an internal battery or phantom power on the console. They tend to be more expensive than their passive counterparts, but they also tend to sound better and have a better transient response. The passive version can be thought of as a simple dumb box. Usually, the only thing you will find inside a passive direct box is an impedance matching transformer. Some DIs will also have a resistive network that will take a speaker level and drop it to a line level, which then can be dropped to a microphone level by the internal transformer.

* * *

Dynamic Mics

The dynamic mic is the basic workhorse of the industry. Most generic all-purpose mics on a music stage are dynamic. They are relatively inexpensive and work on a simple mechanical principal. Sound enters the head of the mic as acoustical energy and moves a diaphragm of plastic or other material which in turn moves a coil. That coil has a stationary magnet at its core, and the movement of the coil produces an electrical signal, thus the transducer converts acoustical energy into electrical. That's just about the whole story! Simple, right?

Modern-day dynamic mics will also contain a transformer that will change the impedance of the mic into a matching balanced impedance for a mixer. The transformer will also serve to isolate the coil from raw voltage when phantom power is applied to a channel.

Moving coil dynamic microphones are a great choice when a strong, all-purpose, rugged, robust mic is needed with good sound. This mic can also be hot-rodded by the manufacturer by using different or stronger magnets. A classic example of this is the Shure Beta series of microphones that use the much stronger neodymium magnet. N-Dyms will typically have a much higher output than a standard rare earth magnet, and they will be able to take more sound pressure as well.

Condenser Mics

Unlike dynamic mics, condenser mics are active microphones. They have internal electronics that must be powered. Condenser mics have built-in preamplifiers that can run off of an internal battery or phantom power. In electronics, before we had capacitors, we had condensers. Condensers essentially do the same job as a capacitor in that it is an electronic device that stores and discharges energy. When we replaced condensers with capacitors, we never stopped referring to a condenser mic as a condenser mic, but in reality, it could be looked at as a capacitor mic.

Essentially the diaphragm is the moving part of the capacitor. Electricity flows across the diaphragm and air pressure changes the value of the capacitor producing an electronic signal. Condenser microphones are much more precise and delicate than their dynamic counterparts. They have a faster transient response which makes them especially well-suited for instruments with delicate high-frequency sound. It also makes them well-suited for picking up quieter instrumentation on stage as well. They also work best for choir microphones. Most lectern microphones today are some form of a condenser mic.

PZM Mics

A PZM microphone is a *Pressure Zone Microphone*. It uses a tiny condenser element pointed straight down at a plate to create a zone of pressure between the element and the plate. The distance between these is very small. If a dynamic magnet type pickup is a microphone, you could consider a PZM a nano-phone.

A PZM microphone differs from other types of mics in that the plate is actually the surface area of the pickup. As such, whatever flat surface the plate lays on becomes the pick up as well. This is why they make great stage microphones for dramas. Essentially any sound hitting the stage will follow the flat surface into the microphone.

In sound reinforcement we see PZM microphones being used in all kinds of creative ways. I have gaff taped them into the internal sides of pianos causing the entire inner body of the piano to become the mic, used them on tabletops to pick up a large amount of bodies at a table, I even once gaff taped a PZM to a drummers chest in the studio because he wanted to hear his snare on the recording like he felt it while sitting at his drum set.

Ribbon Mics
The ribbon mic is a close cousin to the dynamic and condenser mic. It works in the same basic way, but instead of using a diaphragm, it uses a thin metal ribbon. The advantage is that it moves faster and it is more accurate. The downside? It is fragile.

Remember at the beginning of the chapter when I said that you could kill a mic by using an improper mic in an application? I once knew a bass player who was looking for ways to improve his sound. He decided to exchange his Shure SM57 on his loud Ampeg bass rig for a beautiful expensive studio ribbon vocal mic. It sounded amazing! ....for about two minutes. That worked out to about $150 per minute. So, the warning here is to know your microphone types, and use them for their intended purposes.

Tube Microphones
Tube microphones as the name implies use vacuum tubes as the internal electronics. These microphones offer a warm vintage sound that is simply impossible to get with modern active electronic microphones. This is why they have become the choice of home studio and professional studio recording engineers for tracking things like vocals and acoustic guitars. Nothing can warm up your mix like a great tube microphone running through a tube pre-amp. Because they use glass vacuum tubes, they are also fragile compared

to a modern-day electronic microphone. Also because of this, you will seldom see them being used in live sound reinforcement.

Patterns
Any microphone will have a specific pickup pattern. Common patterns include: cardioid, super cardioid, hyper cardioid, omnidirectional, and the figure eight. A cardioid mic pattern will typically allow sound into the front of the mic and reject sound entering from the back. They are well suited for vocal and instrument mics because they will reject sound entering from monitors and the PA system itself. The term cardioid refers to the three-dimensional cardio heart-shaped pattern of the mic.

Omnidirectional mics are well suited for picking up large areas such as room sound. Occasionally they are used in sound reinforcement on things like choirs and overheads but are more common in television and recording because feedback in that application is not an issue. They are also common in test microphones for room analyzation because of their spherical all-direction pattern. You'll probably run into them, but they are not as common as the cardioid.

The figure eight pattern is an option on many studio-grade microphones. They come in handy any time you wish to mic two objects or people with one mic and still need rejection to the sides.

Stereo Mic'ing Rule
There are many instances that you may choose to use more than one microphone and one channel on the console to mic an instrument or group of people. Percussion, for instance, is a very popular place where you will typically use more than one microphone to mic a particular instrument. Good stereo mic placement is essential to get the best quality sound when using more than one microphone on a source. We'll touch on technique in the next chapter, but we'll set a ground rule here before we move on.

The first rule to remember when using multiple microphones to mic a specific instrument is the three to one rule. This rule states that anytime you use more than one microphone to mic a source, each microphone should be three times the distance apart for every one time the distance to what you are mic'ing.

Let's say you have a choir and you have two choir mics that are 3 feet away from your vocalists. The two microphones should then be 9 feet or more apart from each other. This will help eliminate sounds arriving out of phase from your source into the two microphones.

Let's take another example in the percussion area. Let's mic a bar of wind chimes. We are going to use two microphones to stereo mic them. We want to arrange these microphones so we get a good left to right sweep when the percussionist runs his stick across them. The wind chime bar in our example is 2 feet long. We place the first microphone in the left area of the rack about 5 inches off the chimes. This will dictate that there needs to be at least 15 inches distance before the next microphone on the right side. Theoretically, you should have little phase interference as the stick travels from left to right across the chimes.

Another common area would be overheads on a drum kit. In this case, we will use two overhead condensers to mic four cymbals on the set. If you are looking at your drum set from the stage, on the left you will see a ride and a crash. On the right, you will see two smaller cymbals. We will choose to put a microphone over the two on the left and another over the two on the right. We have evenly spaced these microphones between their cymbal pairs in order to pick up both evenly about a foot above. This would dictate that the minimum distance that we will need between the two microphones is 3 feet. It's perfectly fine to go beyond 3 feet if needed as we are only concerned with the minimum distance.

Chapter 13

Mic Technique

Let's look at the various mic'ing techniques that you may encounter while mixing sound. While we may not touch on every single scenario you may run into in the course of your journey behind a console, you should come away with the basic principles needed to mic just about anything you might come across in an effective manner. This chapter will be structured in reference style so you can go back at a later date and brush up on anything you may choose.

Old School Importance
In the late eighties, I trained a young upcoming engineer by the name of Craig Young. Today, Craig is a professional studio engineer and bassist for acts like Elton John, Jewel, Lady Antebellum, and Peter Frampton. Craig started off with me primarily as a monitor engineer and stage tech and learned the professional ropes of mic technique in the trenches from the ground up.

One day Craig walked into a predominant world class recording studio in New York with a client to track some drums and bass for a project. He was met by the studio's systems engineer who received a simple old-school track sheet from Craig.

"This will be a real simple night," Craig told the in-house engineer, "just basic rhythm tracks and a basic mic setup." Craig handed the young engineer his track sheet and the young man simply stared at it with a troubled blank look. After an awkward moment, Craig simply looked at the young man and said, "You've never mic'ed a real drum set before, have you?" The man simply shook his head no.

* * *

As technology grows and real instruments are replaced with loops and plug-ins, it's becoming harder to find engineers that really understand their craft from the ground up. If you are going to be a good engineer, it's imperative to understand the basic mic'ing techniques for any instrument with which you might find yourself presented. Even if your church uses things like electronic drums and keyboards, you never know when you might be facing a guest musician who presents you with a live drum kit or an acoustic piano.

Drum Mic'ing
Acoustic drums present an interesting collection of challenges. There is no overall correct way to mic drums. For instance, the number of microphones can vary from one overhead for the entire kit to every piece mic'ed individually and everything in between. You will have to take many things into account like, what will the volume of the drums be in the room? How critical will isolation be in my application? And, how many mics and channels do I have at my disposal?

The single mic technique involves placing a condenser mic overhead on the kit. The EQ will usually remain fairly flat for this technique as you're wanting to grab the entire kit with a single mic. You can, however, utilize your EQ section to bring out parts of the kit that may otherwise be lost or down in volume. For instance, boosting high frequencies will boost the symbols and high hat, while boosting the low end will favor toms and kick. The mid frequencies will bring out the snare.

Add a second mic and I have found the best overall placement is either in the kick and overhead or kick and snare. Add a third mic and now we can graduate to either kick, snare, overhead, or kick, snare, high hat. The specific combination is really determined by what sounds best for your particular situation, and you may have to try different combinations to answer that question.

Next, we generally move into an entirely mic'ed drum kit. You have three options with toms. You can use one mic per two toms by placing in between, you can mic each individually, or you can use a combination of both, depending on the kit and the amount of available channels and mics.

Kick

When mic'ing a kick drum, remember that the tone of the kick, or it's depth, comes from the shell. Thus you will get a richer sound with your mic set off center. Also know that the center of the drum tends to be rather thin by comparison due to the nulling effect of phase and the fact that the beater hits the drum on its center. The deep tones that a kick produces will not fully develop if the kick is sealed with heads on both sides. To get the lowest tones and the deepest sound out of a kick, you will need a sound hole cut off center in the kick, or in some cases, no outer head at all.

Large diaphragm microphones make an excellent choice for kick drums because they can take a huge amount of sound pressure. The drawback of these mics is that they are a bit on the slow side as the diaphragms are huge and lumbering. Some engineers will compensate for this in highly critical situations by using two kick drum mic channels. One with a large diaphragm mic for the deep tones and one specialty kick drum mic, usually a PZM type, that is specifically designed to deliver great crack in the drum at high sound pressure levels.

Manufactures like Shure have attempted to address these issues with large diaphragm microphones with faster, stronger magnets and specific tuning through selective phase cancellation. The Shure Beta 52 remains a great choice for kicks because it solves many of these problems, but be forewarned, the classic B52 does so by specifically tuning the microphone to the sweet frequencies of a kick drum. The mic will not sound great in hardly anything but a kick. It is a true specialist and should be treated as such.

* * *

Snare

The snare can be mic'ed from the top, just off the head itself. Turn the mic so it captures the snare easily, rejects other toms and the hat, and is located in a place comfortable for the drummer, so he won't whack it in the middle of your worship service. If you're not using a high hat mic, then position the snare mic midway between to pick up both. In some highly critical instances, you may want to add a second snare mic under the snare to pick up more of the snare sound. If you use this method, remember you will need to throw the bottom mic out of phase on your console in order to put the snare sound back into phase.

If this seems confusing to you, let's think about what's happening as the snare is hit. When the top skin of the snare is hit, the head moves in a downward motion. This motion will actually cause the microphone diaphragm to move in the same direction. The bottom snare does the same, moving downward, the problem now is that the lower mic is facing backward to the top. So in effect, when negative pressure is created on the top mic's diaphragm, positive is being created on the bottom, and vice versa. When you throw either mic out of phase with the other, they once again start working as one unit instead of fighting against each other. My personal mic of choice here is a good old Shure SM57 or its Beta version.

High Hat

A good quality condenser mic is in order here. While a dynamic will pick up the brass of a high hat, a condenser is really needed to be fast enough to reproduce its crisp transient response. As for position, point the mic straight down, close to the edge on the top hat. A condenser mic coming in from the side will be overly sensitive to the air that is being created by the top and bottom hat upon closing. This will also help isolate the hat from other cymbal mics, as they will typically be EQ'ed in a similar fashion. The highest of frequencies are being generated at the edge of the hat, and that's what you're looking for! Keep the mic away from the inside portion of the hat as it is generating most of the unwanted harsh brass.

Toms

There is a wide spectrum of great tom mics out there. Generally speaking, they will almost always want to point across the drum head from a *just off the rim* position. Take care to minimize bleed from other parts of the drum kit when placing tom mics. A noise gate will only be so effective if the symbols are practically laying on the tom mics. There are a wide variety of tom mics available to you from small condensers specifically designed for toms to larger dynamics like the trusty Shure SM57.

Overheads

Overhead mics can be an art form. The rule of thumb here is to try to use a good quality condenser mic similar to what you might use on a high hat. Isolation and phase are your two biggest concerns here. If the kit has many cymbals, you might try placing both mics over the kit together in an XY pattern. This will effectively keep sound entering both mics in phase with each other, and it will give you a wide stereo pattern of the entire kit. If you're looking at both of the mics head-on, place one mic in the 4 o'clock position with the other in the 8 o'clock position. Make sure the diaphragms are touching each other in the middle.

If your kit has two distinct sides of cymbals, then you might use a left, right configuration. Just remember the three to one ratio rule of mic'ing which states that if you have two mics in the same area, make sure that each mic is mic'ing its intended target, with the other mic three times the distance away. In other words, if the left mic is six inches from a target cymbal, make sure the right mic is at least eighteen inches away from the same cymbal, and vice versa. If you're a foot off, make sure the other is three off, etc.

A kit may be as simple as a crash and a ride. These are probably the easiest kits to get to sound great because each cymbal gets one mic. No guessing, no experimentation, it's just throw and go! When mic'ing an individual cymbal, take note to mic it close to the outer edge. Cymbals use the inner portion to produce the lower brass tones and the sizzle is found at the edge. Every sound engineer knows how easy it is to get brass into a sound system mix. It's everywhere. It bleeds into all your drum channels and it's plenty loud in a small room with no amplification at all. High-end sizzle is a different story. High frequencies are fragile, and you need to use every trick in your arsenal to accentuate that sizzle and reject the harsh brass.

Electric Guitar
There are a few secrets that you need to know about mic'ing guitar amplifiers that will have you mic'ing like a pro. The first thing that you need to be aware of is where your speaker is exactly in the cabinet. This can be difficult at times because some grills will not allow you to see exactly where the speaker is. With most guitar amplifiers you can look in the back of the cabinet to see the speakers exact location.

The speaker itself in a guitar amplifier cabinet will produce different parts of the guitar tone, depending on the part of the speaker. High frequencies are produced toward the middle of the speaker, and warmer frequencies are produced more toward the edge. If your guitar sound is too bright, try moving your microphone more towards the edge of the speaker to begin with in order to warm it up. If a guitar is not biting enough, try moving it more toward the center of the speaker. Two inches distance will make a huge difference in the sound. Experiment and start off with the best possible sound before applying any EQ back at the console.

If you are short a mic stand, you can always use the poor man's mic stand technique when it comes to mic'ing a guitar cabinet. In this technique, you loop the mic cable through the handle of the cabinet to hold it in place and drape it down the front of the cabinet. Plug in the microphone so the microphone is pointing right at the edge of the speaker facing down. You can still adjust the sound by moving the microphone back-and-forth on the speaker, and while this technique works very well, a microphone stand will still give you the best sound, and as such, this method should only be used as a last resort.

It has been my experience over the years that guitars will start off too bright as opposed to not bright enough. Therefore I usually start with my microphone at the edge of the speaker and move it in as needed.

Most dynamic microphones have a proximity effect that will give you a low-end boost if the microphone is within an inch and a half of the grill of the cabinet. Therefore I place my mic about an inch from the grill. If you pull it back, the sound will become more airy, but you will also have more bleed into the microphone from other instruments onstage. It's a balancing act.

If your guitarist is playing through a stereo cabinet or has two cabinets that he is running with a stereo processor, mic them in stereo. Pan your two channels hard left and right in this circumstance. This will provide a huge difference in your sound and it is well worth eating the second channel on your soundboard to do so.

If you have two guitarists on stage at the same time, you can gain more separation between the two distinct guitars by following any one of a few simple techniques. The first technique is to simply offset the panning on the two guitars ever so simply. Take the two guitars and pan them at 10 o'clock and 2 o'clock. You're not looking for big stereo sound here, you're just looking for a little added separation of the two.

If one of your guitarists is playing in stereo you can simply leave him at left and right and the other guitar straight up. There will be much more separation in the sound than if you had two mono guitars panned straight up.

If you have two mono guitars you can always leave the lead panned straight up and take the rhythm guitar and convert it into a stereo mix and pan it left and right. If you just read that and you're scratching your head thinking to yourself *how do I make a mono guitar stereo?* You'll have to wait a few chapters until we get to *engineering secrets revealed*. Have I piqued your curiosity?

Acoustic Guitar
For acoustic guitars, I prefer to mic them in the studio and use a direct box live. A microphone will give the acoustic guitar a more airy sound. In many ways a more natural sound. However, microphones can be problematic live because of monitors. An acoustic guitar is also a relatively weak instrument as far as output goes compared to other electronic instruments on the stage.

When using the direct box live, I prefer an active direct box to a passive one. An active direct box has a better transient response. Guitar strings, especially new guitar strings, will have a very fast transient response. An active direct box can keep up with these whereas a passive direct box will tend to lag a little behind.

If you do choose to use a microphone live instead of a direct box, choose a condenser mic with a cardioid pattern to avoid bleed from the monitors as much as possible. When mic'ing an acoustic live, in-ear monitors are your friend.

You will want to place your microphone at the guitar's sound hole about four to six inches off. The trick is to get as close to the guitar as possible without your musician hitting it. Remember that guitarists will naturally move about and your microphone will vary up to a foot in location during your performance, so you may want to consider compressing an acoustic channel slightly when using a microphone. This is the second reason that a condenser microphone works better than a dynamic microphone in this application.

Bass Guitar
Like the acoustic guitar, my preference here is to use a direct box. If a DI is not readily available, you can mic the speaker cabinet. The same rules for mic'ing a guitar amplifier apply here. You will get a very different sound from a mic as compared to the DI. Many engineers will use both and blend the two to get the best of both worlds. Using both simultaneously will also give you a fail-safe in case you lose a channel for some reason.

Vocals
Vocals can be frustrating because they are the one thing on stage for which you cannot take actual responsibility, and the vocals can make or break your mix. As a control freak, there's nothing that's going to bug you more than that!

The best thing you can do here is to be an educator with your vocalists. Teach them to stay on their microphones! Typical vocal microphones have a proximity effect. This means that they will have a warmth and volume boost within two inches of the mic. As the performer moves away from the microphone both warmth and volume drop dramatically and proportionally.

I teach my vocalists to actually touch their microphone with their lips when they are singing. One graphic example you can do for them is to demonstrate that for every inch that they pull away from the microphone, they will cause a drop in monitor volume by about half. I will get their monitor sounding good and loud and then I will put the microphone in front of their mouth and tell them to start counting to 20. I will warn them not to change their volume at all as they are counting and tell them to listen closely to their monitor. As they are counting I will pull the microphone back one inch and say, "One inch." After a couple of numbers I will pull it back another inch and say, "Two inches," and so on out to about six inches. By the time they get to six inches, they realize that they can no longer hear themselves and it serves as a graphic example of proximity effect.

If I am teaching a class of say six or so worship team members, while I am talking to them I will simply start pulling my microphone back from my mouth making sure that they can still hear just enough to know what I'm saying. I will point out how much volume is lost with these simple movements. These graphic examples should serve to improve their future mic technique.

Choir
Choirs are pretty straightforward. The only recommendation I would make with choirs is to use the same type of mics throughout. We will typically use condenser mics when it comes to choirs. Dynamics will work as well but certainly not as good as condensers.

Choir mics will either be done on a permanent basis with hanging microphones or you will have temporary microphones on stands. Evenly space the microphones throughout your choir and adhere to the three to one rule. Use the fewest amount of microphones needed to get the job done, but use enough microphones to be able to hear all of the sections of the choir equally.

Percussion
You will do some of your most creative mic'ing with percussion. There are two methods for mic'ing percussion, depending on the

number of microphones and channels that you have available. If you have a small number of microphones and few open channels, then you'll want to get by with the smallest amount of mics as possible. If you have a lot of channels open with which to work, and a lot of mics in your arsenal, try to be as creative as possible with stereo mic'ing.

Percussion is one area that will lend itself to wide stereo panning. This is so because you can lose little parts of the percussion if you're way off to one side of the auditorium and still hear a great worship team mix. But for those in the center of the auditorium, you can really put some spice on your mix here that will cause interest for your listener.

When I am mic'ing up percussion with limited channels, it's not uncommon for me to use one microphone for any two adjacent drums or congas. If I have an area that a lot of percussive instruments are grouped together like cymbals and timbales, I may use a single area mic overhead. If I have very few mics available to designate to the percussion section, I may simply take two microphones and do a stereo overhead in the general area picking up the entire percussion area.

If I have an abundance of mics and stands in my percussion area, I will treat everything individually and go to town with stereo mic'ing. I may draw the line with a toy table, simply putting a stereo mic or two mics in an XY configuration over the toy tray to pick up the nuances of the percussionist.

I always go out of my way to let the percussionist know that he is being mic'ed in stereo. That way, when he wants to, he can move his shakers and toys from left to right around in the stereo spectrum. You can have a fun relationship with your percussionist when your percussionist understands the dynamics of your mic'ing scheme.

Horns
Horns are typically loud and need little amplification in the

small room. Having said that, even in the small room there are times when a saxophonist, for instance, may play softly. I will tend to mic my horns with a dynamic mic like an SM57 on a stand in front of the instrument or use a clip-on microphone on the bell of the horn. Many horn players will own their own rigs and this will make your life easy because all you have to do is plug in an XLR cable and go.

Leslie Cabinets

Many traditional churches will still use Leslie speakers. A Leslie cabinet is a cabinet with two rotating horn speakers. It's the classic tremolo effect still heard in recordings today. Typically there are two rotating horns in a Leslie cabinet, a high-frequency horn on the top and a low-frequency horn on the bottom. Motors rotate these horns around at a speed determined by the player. The player is able to speed up the horns separate from each other, producing the different rotating speaker sounds.

I will mic a Leslie cabinet in one of two ways. If I am limited to two channels I will put a dynamic mic like an SM57 in the top cut out for the top horn and another SM57 down below for the low-frequency horn. If I have the luxury of mic'ing a Leslie in stereo, I will use three microphones. In this case, I will use 2 SM57s in the top speaker for my left and right. I will take one SM57 on each side of the horn, on the far left and far right. I will pan them hard left and hard right in the PA. A third microphone pans straight up capturing the bottom bass horn. This is by far the best sounding way to do a Leslie cabinet.

Stereo Mic'ing Techniques

There are two basic techniques for stereo mic placement. The first technique involves two microphones separated by distance. We see this method routinely utilized in places like the overhead mics on the drum kit. Other places you can see this technique in use is on choirs, percussion areas, and in the individual mic'ing of separate guitar amplifiers.

The second method involves using two matched microphones in close proximity. This method works great if you are mic'ing something that is relatively close in area. This method has the advantage of keeping your sound in phase between the left and right channels. While the microphones can vary in their configuration a bit, this is also commonly known as XY mic'ing. The key to this mic'ing method is keeping the diaphragms of the two microphones on the same plane. Because they are in the same location, sound will hit the two microphones at the same time, keeping the left and right signal in phase with each other.

You will do this method in one of two ways generally. The first method we will look at is the X method. In this method, you will take the first microphone and point it directly at your source like an acoustic guitar. The second microphone will mount on a second stand directly above the first mic at a ninety-degree angle with the two diaphragms crossing each other like an X or more accurately, a plus. These microphones are then panned left and right and brought up into the PA.

In the Y technique, the two microphones cross each other's diaphragms like a plus just like before, only both microphones are now facing forward towards the area that you are mic'ing. The pattern of pick up is like a Y. This method can be used overhead on drum kits when there are many cymbals on the kit and you have to get an overall in-phase mix of the entire area. It's also a good technique to use in small areas that can be separated into a stereo mix like a toy table in a percussion area.

* * *

Faith Comes by Hearing

Chapter 14

Tonality

The ability to perceive, understand, and effectively work with tonality and frequency is fundamental in your quest to be a good engineer. Frequency is the paint on your canvas. As an artist, you must have an effective knowledge of how those colors mix, interact, and affect your final outcome. This is why we use phrases like *coloration* when we want to point out how a sound or a particular piece of gear is adding its own sound or artifact to the mix.

In this chapter, we're going to go over some of the basic instruments that you'll likely encounter in church sound (and some you might not). We'll look at the frequency range that they occupy, and we'll discuss the areas in their range that are key areas to address in a mix.

Kick

The overall EQ of the kick drum has three basic areas of importance. The fullness of the shell of the kick happens from about 100 Hz to around 300 Hz. There is usually an abundance of these frequencies in your mix and in your room. It is not uncommon for me to pull back frequencies in these areas. If I'm starting off with a great kick to begin with, and you look at my channel card, you'll probably find some frequencies pulled back around 120 Hz. That frequency may differ in my mix in conjunction with the resonant frequency in a room. This is where booming takes place, and if your room is boomy at 120 Hz, you'll probably be pulling your kick drum back in that region as well.

The low-end punch in the kick is around 50 to 60 Hz. I will typically end up boosting in this area somewhere. There is usually a sympathetic relationship between what I am boosting in this region and what I am taking out in the region mentioned previously.

The next area of interest is the *crack* of the kick. This is where you're going to get your definition out of the kick and allow the audience to hear the kick as well as feel it. You will find the sweet spot somewhere between 1K and 3K that when boosted, will add a little bit of a metallic crack to the kick drum sound. It will sound a little unusual on its own, but once you hear it in a mix, your kick drum will come alive and sound quite natural.

Snare
The snare does not have as many variables as the kick, or at least it is generally not as drastic as the kick in tonal variance when it comes to being EQ'ed. The areas of the snare that we look at generally are its ring and its crack.

The ring of the snare generally occurs in the 900 Hz region, give or take 100 Hz. The whack of the snare happens at around 3K. Fullness in the snare can happen between 120 and 200 Hz, but if it's a good sounding snare to begin with, you will find that you won't do much EQ'ing at all to get a snare to sound great.

The secret with the snare is to use the right tool for the right job. In other words, don't try to get a deep snare sound out of a piccolo snare. A snare should sound like itself through of PA. We do some pretty heavy altering at times with kick drums and toms to get them to sound great through PAs, but by contrast, if you're starting off with a great snare to begin with, it should sound just like its unamplified self through the PA, only louder.

The lowest frequencies are usually high passed out of the snare as you don't need any of the low toms or kick drum coming through the snare mic. The same can be said for high frequencies. We don't need cymbals bleeding through the snare mic, although adding a little in those frequencies can improve the snap of a snare with an old head.

* * *

High Hat and Cymbals

The First order of business with high hat and symbol channels is to dump the frequencies that are either not present or are unwanted. Symbols and high hats produce a lot of brass frequencies that will tend to bleed into all of the other microphones on the kit. We do not need to reproduce these frequencies as they do quite a fine job of adding harshness to your mix on their own.

What we do need to amplify through the PA system is the high-frequency sizzle of these instruments. I will typically listen to a hi-hat or overhead channel and begin by high passing as much of the unwanted lower frequencies out of the mic as possible. The thought here is that you do not need any low frequencies from anything else in close proximity bleeding into those microphones.

After I've removed the brass, I will sometimes give a little bump in the high frequency, somewhere between 5 and 15K. Modern-day sound systems and speakers do not suffer from the same problems with reproducing high-frequency as compared to the speakers of the past. New materials found in horns have made speaker cabinets far more efficient at reproducing high-frequency, therefore you will find that you no longer have to boost these frequencies as much as we did in days past. Be careful here, adding a lot of high-frequency into your mix is a sure way to fatigue the ears of your listener after a short amount of time.

Hi-hat and symbol EQ'ing today has been more about getting rid of the frequencies that you don't want than boosting the frequencies that you do. Generally speaking today if we are greatly boosting high frequencies in this area, it is probably an attempt to compensate for poor speakers, poor acoustics, poor microphones, or poor instruments.

A well-placed proper microphone will usually provide you with all of the high-frequency you need for an overhead or symbol. If you're finding that you're grabbing the EQ knob to boost in these areas, it would be a good idea to ask yourself why. The problem may be solved by replacing the mic, or simply moving the mic to a better location.

Toms

A tom tom's tonal range is going to fall from about 60 Hz on the low end to about 6K on the high. Above 6K is generally nothing but cymbal bleed so use caution in boosting those frequencies. Boosting the lowest frequencies in the 60 to 100 Hz range will boost the perceived low frequency of the tom. Generally, the only time we're doing that is on the larger toms like floor toms.

Like the kick drum, toms can drone a bit in the 120 to 300 Hz range, and this is commonly seen when the drummer is playing with dead heads. The crack of the tom is generally in the 2K to 5K range. Slightly boosting these frequencies will cause the tom to stand out in the mix when struck. Again you never want to add a great amount of these high frequencies as you will also unwittingly start turning up the brass of the cymbals in that range.

Bass

An electric bass will have a far greater frequency range than one might initially think. Your primary frequency range of focus is from 60 Hz on the low end to 6K on the high.

Bass guitars can produce sustained low-frequency notes that can get out of control in a room quickly. This is one of those areas where it is imperative to know the resonant frequency of your room. If your room is muddy in the low end, and the drums and bass guitar are adding to that mud, reducing the frequency of the room's resonant frequency in the bass will do much to combat the problem in your mix.

Acoustic Guitar

The acoustic guitar falls into the 200 Hz to 6K region. You are looking for an acoustic guitar that sounds great acoustically on its own. Secondly, you are looking for one that sounds good relatively flat through the PA system. If you have both of these elements married with an accomplished acoustic guitar player, your life with an acoustic guitar is going to be relatively easy. Lose any one of those elements and you're going to have to do some engineering.

If you have an acoustic guitar that sounds great live, without any amplification, yet sounds poor through a PA system, the problem is probably not in the guitar itself but in its pickup or electronics. Generally speaking the less EQ'ing you have to do to an acoustic guitar the better.

If your acoustic sounds poor through the PA system, you will have to listen to it critically and try to compensate with equalization. If it's too bright, you're going to have to lose brightness in the 1K to 5K region. If it's too boomy you're going to have to lose boominess in and around the 200 to 300 Hz region. If it's not warm, you will have to you add artificial warmth in the low end in the 100 to 200 Hz region. And of course, if it's dull and lifeless, you will have to add a bit of high-frequency to it to bring out presence. This can usually be found in the 3K to 10K range.

Electric Guitar

In many ways, an electric guitar is easier to deal with than an acoustic. It's louder and often times, a little more forgiving and a little less fragile. The same frequencies present in the acoustic are applicable to the electric guitar with one major difference. An electric guitar has the added element of crunch. Never underestimate the excess or lack of power or crunch in your electric guitar. Generally, this crunch can be found around 2K. Too much and your entire mix will be harsh and fatiguing. Not enough and your entire mix will lack power and energy.

Piano

Theoretically, the piano keyboard spans the entire human listening spectrum from 40 Hz out to about 16K. I say theoretically because not all piano keyboards are created equal. Most keyboards that I run into in church settings are what I would classify as mediocre. The vast majority of pianos and keyboards fall into this middle ground of acceptable fidelity.

If you have an old piano or keyboard in your church, you know the frustration of having to deal with an instrument that is way too dull or way too tinny. When you get the opportunity to work on the high-end side of the spectrum with an expensive grand, you will appreciate the difference.

Like anything in audio, pianos tend to reproduce their mid-range frequencies the loudest, with the ends of the spectrum both low and high being the hardest to reproduce. This is why when mic'ing a stand-up piano it's always best to move your microphones closer to the far left and right of the soundboard than placing them in the middle. Those center frequencies will be loud enough, but it will be the outer ends of your audio spectrum that you will have the hardest time reproducing as loud as everything else.

Keys
Modern-day keyboards are nothing more than electronic simulations of pianos and synthesizers. As such, the same rules apply as far as frequency. They can be a little bit better when it comes to the low and high frequencies being as loud as the mid-range, but they will still tend to have a louder mid-range than the ends of the spectrum.

Cheaper keyboards will often need to be brightened up a bit as they will not be as live in the 5K region as an expensive counterpart. An expensive counterpart will also have a tighter low-end and while you can boost the low end of the cheap keyboard, I'm afraid there's no real way to engineer it to sound as tight. The old adage rings true here that *you get what you pay for*.

Horns
Brass actually has a fairly wide range with most of the energy falling between 60 Hz and 6K. Most problems with these instruments will occur in the mid-range. Honk resides at about 500 Hz and harshness lives in the 1 to 2K region. It's not uncommon for

me to warm up a saxophone in the lower 250 Hz range, and on the rare occasion, I have been known to add a little back into a saxophone at 5K, especially when it is more of a lead instrument onstage.

Strings

Strings will run the full spectrum from 60 Hz out to 16K. Typically with strings, if you're doing a lot of EQ'ing it's due to a poor pick up in an instrument. A great sounding instrument played by an accomplished player will usually not require a ton of EQ when properly mic'ed. We can high pass the instrument to get rid of anything below its lowest frequencies, and I will low-pass an instrument to take out any of the high-frequency that is not needed.

Pipe Organ

Even more so than strings, a pipe organ is as close to a full spectrum instrument as you will get. Pipe organs have the ability to produce notes down to 20 Hz and have a high-frequency range out to 16K. A pipe organ built into a cathedral is typically not mic'ed through the PA. It is a unique standalone device and in many cathedrals it is in fact a part of the construction of the building itself.

The Male Voice

Of all of the things that you will mic as an engineer, you would think that the simplest task would be the vocal. It's a simple mic on a stand in front of an individual onstage. Put the mic in front of the mouth, and turn it up in the system. How hard can it be?

Actually, the human voice is the most difficult instrument on stage to get right. There are a few reasons for this, first being that this is not a manufactured instrument. Every voice is a unique creation with qualities unique to each and every one.

Secondly, the human voice is the instrument onstage with which we are the most familiar. Our brain hears the human voice almost every day of our lives. Because of this familiarity, we are so acquainted with the human voice that we have the most critical ear when it comes to its sound. When it comes to the voice, our brain is not easily fooled. If a voice does not sound natural, our brain will immediately recognize that fact. A lay person in our audience might not have the expertise to know what's wrong with the sound of the human voice or what's off about it, but their brain will recognize that there's something wrong or different with the sound. That makes getting the voice right a critical task at any soundcheck.

The frequency range of the male voice runs from about 60 Hz to 10K. Because all voices are different, the sweet spot or range within this spectrum will shift throughout, depending on the singer's particular range and style.

The lowest usable frequencies in the male voice are generally found down in the 120 Hz region. Over my career in sound, I've had the pleasure of working with two artists whose voices dove below 60 Hz. The first was Richard Kiel, the actor best known for playing the character Jaws in the James Bond films and J. D. Sumner with The Stamps Quartet. At the time that I worked with J. D., he was in the Guinness Book of World Records for the lowest recorded human bass note on record. Low frequency in the 120 Hz to 250 Hz range may need to be increased to add thickness to a voice or subtracted to take away any boominess.

Vocals are always high passed. Most of my vocal channels will have the high pass filter set anywhere between 120 and 160 Hz.

The midrange of the male voice falls from 400 Hz to 800 Hz. Because of this, you will find that most of the energy resides within this range as well. These frequencies seldom need boosting in the PA, any more than 1K ever needs boosting on a third-octave graphic equalizer on your entire house. Generally, there is not a problem reproducing these frequencies. There is usually an abundance of midrange to deal with. Because of this, it is not uncommon to lose frequencies around 600 Hz in the vocal range. Small dips here will usually clean up your vocal channels, balancing out the frequency response of your vocalist.

* * *

Presence and harshness are found in the 5K region. If the vocalist is piercing, a small dip in this area will take care of that. If a vocalist is lacking in high-frequency definition, a small raise somewhere between 6K and 15K will add airiness and definition.

The Female Voice

The female voice has a very similar high-end characteristic when compared to the male vocal. This, of course, will depend on the male's high-end range as it can vary greatly, but generally speaking very few male or female voices will have any information above 16K. In fact, most of the high-end region for both is found from 5 to 8K. The low-frequency end is where the two vary greatly. Female voices will seldom have a great amount of energy below 250 Hz and the majority of the low end will be much higher compared to their male counterparts. Typically a female vocal mic will be hi passed higher than a male.

Spoken Word

EQ for the spoken word is very similar to EQ for a vocal mic. The major difference here is the type of microphone that is being used, as head-worn mics are usually the best choice for a pastor delivering a sermon. The first thing you'll want to do with a spoken word microphone is to get rid of any unneeded low-frequency energy as well as high-frequency. Past that you will likely have to equalize down the mid-range portion of the voice in the 500 to 800 Hz region.

The Elephant in the Room

As we were going through all of these frequencies one thing should become quite apparent. When it comes to your mix, there is an elephant in the room. That elephant's name is 1K.

When you add multiple instruments into a mix they will all cause frequency overlap. The center of the audio spectrum in the 600 to 1K region will overlap with almost every microphone you add to the mix. Because of this scenario, every time you add another element into a PA mix, you are adding more energy in this region. You may start off with a very flat EQ on your house PA, but you may find after adding 12 to 24 channels through a system that your house EQ is in need of some lowering of this range.

Every PA can produce 1K because it is in the middle of the audio spectrum, away from the extreme edges. Because of its location, it is the easiest of tones to reproduce. You will have to keep an eye on this area throughout your mix to make sure that you are not overloading the mid range.

Chapter 15

Getting The Mix

Now we're going to go over the basics of getting a good mix up and going. Every engineer is different, and there are no absolute correct ways of getting the job done. As I have, over time, you will also develop your own unique style. Think of this chapter simply as an opportunity to look over the shoulder of a veteran professional to see how he does it. As I go along, I'll point out a few alternatives to the way I do things, and give you my reasons behind my particular methods.

Over time you too will develop your own unique habits and rituals. Like any other skill, you will develop your own individual style and rhythm to setting up your mix, regardless of what kind of music it is or what type of event. These methods and rhythms will become second nature in time.

Setting up the Console
A big advantage of today's digital consoles is the ability to create pre-made templates for your mix starting points. One might think that resetting your console to the factory reset would be a good starting point for setting up a mix, but with most consoles, you'd be wrong. A factory default is just that. Its an all-encompassing method of completely zeroing out a console. A completely zeroed board is not an efficient way to start a mix. By default, you will want some generic things already in your console every time you begin a mix. This will give you a head start every time you set out to start a fresh mix or setup.

As a rule of practice, I will carry a USB drive with me with some pre-programmed starting points for the various consoles I work on. In a church setting, you'll likely have various starting points saved for different types of services and worship team configurations, but you'll also want to carry a basic console setup for those times when you're starting a new project from scratch.

I will typically set up any console in the same generic way. Remember that with a digital console, all you have to do generally is to set up one channel strip, then copy and paste it to the rest of the board.

By default, many consoles will start with the gain in the far left position or totally off. I prefer the gain's starting position straight up in the twelve o'clock position. This allows me to see when there is a signal present on a channel before I start making adjustments. This position is high enough for most signals to allow you to see it on the channel meter, but in most cases, it won't be so high as to distort or clip the channel.

The next step is to set common channel strip buttons to the on position. For me, this includes the high pass filter, the EQ section, and the channel compressor. If the manufacturer mutes the input channel by default, I will unmute it. By default, consoles will start with EQs set flat and aux sends turned all the way down. This is fine, however, some consoles will also have on/off switches for every aux send. When this is the case, I will turn all the aux buttons on. After setting up the first channel exactly the way you want your zeroed board to be, copy and paste that channel to all of the mic inputs on the console.

Manufacturers starting with the EQ buttons off is really a throwback to the days of analog consoles. Back in that era, the button would reroute the audio signal completely around a large amount of circuitry in the board. When the EQ button was engaged, the audio would travel through a large electronic neighborhood that added noise and distortion, even if you didn't turn any knobs in that section.

In today's digital environment, there is no audio going through these sections. The control surface is simply telling the processors in the board how to process the signal, so there is no appreciable difference to the audio signal whether or not that section is engaged. Starting with the button engaged saves time, and lessens the likelihood of making the mistake of turning knobs that are not doing anything because the section was off.

Other template time savers might include patching EQs on the board's outputs and monitor sends. I like to start with an assortment of basic effects on my console that might include a combination of gated reverb, short reverb, long reverb, a chorus, and a delay line. I also allow for a playback of an audio device such as an iPod or equivalent playback devices such as a computer or CD player.

Once your template is ready, give it a name, and save it to your console as well as to a personal device like a thumb drive. After all, backing up your console to your console's memory does nothing for you if your console has a complete memory failure. You'll then be happy that you had the foresight to save a backup off surface.

Everything Starts with Gain
One of the prevalent mistakes I see in audio mixing is people ignoring the input gain. Typically, I'll get a call from a client who just can't seem to get a signal loud enough in a main or monitor mix. Your entire mix, from the consoles standpoint, starts with the input gain knob.

All audio signals are different in level. Some are faint; some are incredibly strong. The input trim is your method of pre-balancing these signals in order to get the most out of your mix. It's also the knob that will give you the best signal to noise ratio throughout the rest of your console when it's properly set. Think of it this way, if your EQ controls equalize and balance your tone, your input gain knob equalizes and balances the relative volume of everything entering the console.

*　*　*

Engineers will set this gain stage by one of two methods. The first method involves turning up all the faders on the console to unity and then gaining up each individual channel until you achieve your mix. For this type of engineer, they will most likely build their zero template with the gains at the far left or off position. This method allows the engineer to see at a glance which faders he has moved during a mix. These engineers are a little on the OCD side as they really like to see all their faders in a nice straight line. While this method is not wrong as long as nothing is clipping, I prefer a method that has the upside of allowing you to get every last ounce of sweetness out of each instrument and squeeze every ounce of clarity out of your console.

With my method, I will start my soundcheck of a channel by having the musician play, and I will gain that channel up until I see a clip light on the strip. I will then back the gain down a number until the clip light never comes back on. I'll set this gain stage without raising my fader on the strip, essentially setting the gain *blind*. During the rest of the soundcheck or service, if I see a clip light tickle, I'll back it down another half number or just a squeeze.

This method will assure my mix the best signal to noise ratio. That is to say, it will feed the console with the hottest signal with the lowest noise possible. If your console has a very weak signal coming in and you're using the consoles electronics to amplify it, the noise floor is going to come up with the signal proportionally. If your signal is hot to begin with, you won't have to rely on the consoles electronics to amplify it as much. So keep those gains up, but don't turn on the red lights on the channel strip.

Ideally, I try to keep my faders between half up and unity. Most consoles will have a zero point of reference on the fader that we call unity. Theoretically, at unity, the console is not amplifying the signal and in turn, is not amplifying the noise floor of the input. If I can't raise my fader to at least half, only then will I turn the gain down a bit to get it to fall into a range that will give me more mix-ability.

* * *

EQ

After the input gain is set, you're off to the task of getting the input to sound as good as it can. There are no hard and fast rules here as to what channels to work on first. I will usually start with whoever is ready. Drums are a good place to start as it usually takes the most time, and your other musicians will tend to get ready for sound check a little faster if they've noticed that the process has begun. Again, if your drummer's not ready, there's no fast rule that says you have to wait until he is. Simply move on to someone else.

The first thing I will do is roll up my high pass filter. A high pass filter will do exactly as the name implies. It will pass all of the high frequencies above the frequency it is set at. It is also sometimes referred to as a low cut filter.

The high pass filter will take out all of the unwanted low-frequency material found on the channel. This could include wind noise, breath noise, the rumble of cars passing, or ambient sounds like air conditioning or heating. The method here is to simply start turning it up until you start hearing it affect the sound that you want to keep. Then back it down a bit. The mentality is, if you can't hear anything below a certain frequency in the instrument or voice, then you don't want to amplify that range.

After getting that out of the way, listen for any frequencies that are standing out in a bad way. It's always better to cut than boost when it comes to EQ. Now if you need to add something, like bite, or presence, or warmth, now's the time to do it.

Getting the Mix

Once everything has been EQ'ed, I will generally set everyone's monitors before actually doing the house mix. We'll go over that in detail in the monitor world chapter.

In a good environment, I will typically start with the drums, then add bass, then the lead instruments, then the rest of the instruments, then the main vocals, and finally the backing vocals. If

I'm in a particularly loud room with poor acoustics, I will sometimes drop back from a fidelity based mix to a survival mix. In this case, I would get my vocals intelligible and then only add into the PA the things that absolutely have to be there. There may be times when your environment will require something in between.

Sledgehammers vs. Precision Screwdrivers

If you've ever had the opportunity to look over the shoulder of a professional engineer at an arena show, you likely saw an engineer making minute occasional movements on the faders, changes so small that you were quite possibly unable to actually even hear what he was doing. This is quite normal and should be your eventual objective by service time.

As a soundcheck begins, you will be reaching into your virtual tool bag to pull out the big tools. Initially, you'll use hammers, picks, and jackhammers in order to make big changes to get things in proximity to something that resembles a mix.

As your soundcheck progresses, your movements will naturally become smaller and more precise as the mix gets closer and closer to what you need it to be. Soundcheck for you is officially over once you've reached a point of making very small movements on the control surface.

By the time that your service has begun, you will be down to pulling out precision tools from your bag. Your changes will become miniscule and at times, inaudible to a casual observer. If I am at an event and hear big changes coming from the house mix, I know that that engineer has not had an opportunity to conduct a proper soundcheck.

Seasoning

Typically I'm not adding any reverb or other seasonings to my mix until I have a good mix up and running. Then I can start to do the small tweaks that will improve it and put my signature on it. I also wait until this stage so I will have a good indication of what I can get away with adding in a particular room as you won't be able to add a great amount of effects in a reflective environment.

Volume
Volume plays an important roll in setting up your mix. When we are working on individual channels, we will typically raise that channel slightly in volume in order to better hear the nuances of the changes we're making. Then we lower the channel 3 dB or so back into the mix to see what it sounds like with everything else.

There is a correlation between volume and EQ with the human ear. It's not uncommon for you to boost a particular frequency even further once a channel has been brought back down in volume and dropped into a mix. Frequency volume will interact and can mask as you assemble a mix, so don't be surprised when a particular channel sounds great on its own but gets lost or muddied in a mix.

Order
Most engineers will painstakingly drag through one channel at a time. While there's ample reason for that, and while I am generally the same way, I have learned a few time-saving tips over the years from working festivals that speed up my soundcheck workflow.

One area is in the drum check. Instead of having a drummer give me a steady kick for minutes on end while I tweak, I will generally start off with telling the drummer to, "Give me a simple kick, snare, high hat beat." I will then work on all three channels simultaneously. This method works great for several reasons.

First off, I'm not going to have a bored drummer on the other end of my console hitting his drums in a drab, dead manor. A drummer will tend to give you actual concert levels on his hits if he's actually playing a beat. The trick here is to keep him on a simple beat, so you actually have the time to hear the individual hits and adjust them accordingly. Explain to him what you are listening for so he can give you an appropriate slow, solid, sharp beat.

* * *

Secondly, this method works because the kick, the snare, and the high hat all sound quite different. They each fall into their own respective frequency ranges on the kit and it's usually very easy for you to pick them all apart from each other while you're EQ'ing and balancing.

Lastly, these parts of the drum kit are played together as the core sound of the kit most of the time, so you'll be miles ahead in your soundcheck by following this simple method. After all, what good is it to put a noise gate on a kick if you don't know if a snare is going to trigger it?

Toms are a different story as they have a different sound signature characteristic. Toms, as well as cymbals, are the parts of the drum kit that use decay as part of their sound. As such, I will check them individually as I am both EQ'ing the sound of the initial tom and shaping the decay sound of the tom separately.

With cymbals, I generally high pass them quite high until I can only hear the sizzle from them, then add those channels into the overall mix sparingly as the kit is being played, and only as needed. The trick here is to just introduce enough sizzle into your mix to be able to hear them. The room and other mics on the stage will do the rest just from bleed.

Next, I will typically add bass to complete my rhythm section. At this point, you will have the skeletal structure of your mix, and it's time to start hanging organs onto the bones. Add your instruments like guitars and keys and lastly vocals. If your mix is drowning your vocals, bring instruments down rather than turning vocals up.

Balance
The finality of your mix is its overall balance. Nothing jumping out and nothing lost. Once you have a good mix achieved, critically listen for any part becoming masked. Can you understand the

vocals? Can you feel the low end comfortably without feeling overwhelmed by it? Is there harshness?

Now's the time to make those changes that will balance out your final product and remember, it's seldom a matter of making things louder to hear something that is lost. More often than not, it is about turning something down that has become too loud in the mix or EQ'ing out a frequency that is masking an underlying sound.

Chapter 16

Effects

The use of creative effects in sound can be looked at in the same way that we look at seasoning in cooking. A little goes a long way. Just enough seasoning will create a culinary masterpiece, while over-doing it will ruin dinner.

The use of precise use of functional effects will help shape the overall sound of distinct pieces or an entire mix. In this chapter, we will take a look at both.

An effect is essentially any device or software plug-in that alters, or as the name implies, *affects* your signal. In the early days of sound these where standalone boxes that would be plugged into the signal chain at various points. Today effects more often than not tend to be of the digital software variety. They are either plug-ins that can be installed in the signal path via computer software or simply electronic circuits within a console or processor.

Many of today's modern consoles will have a variety of effects built into every channel for processing each input individually. The earliest consoles in sound reinforcement were really nothing more than a volume matrix. These consoles would have six or eight microphone inputs that would be mixed down to one output, and essentially they were simply boxes with knobs on them. It's hard to imagine a huge festival like Woodstock in the sixties being mixed on a number of these types of consoles strapped together without any type of effects whatsoever, but essentially that's what they had to work with.

The first onboard effects to be added to consoles were EQ sections. When they started building bigger consoles for large-scale sound reinforcement purposes, the need to be able to shape the tone of each channel became apparent and these were the first effects to be added to boards. Today's modern consoles go far beyond simple EQ, with various effect processing built into every channel including compressors for every input and noise gates as well.

These devices can affect an individual channel or in many cases, be applied to an entire mix. A compressor can be used to limit the output of a monitor mix in order to protect it. A graphic EQ can be used on an overall house mix to help shape it, etc.

Over the years, manufacturers have come out with all kinds of crazy new effects. Tone shapers, pitch transposers, aural exciters, and a number of esoteric voodoo boxes are out there to choose from, but there is a relatively small variety of everyday staple devices with which you should be intimately familiar with as an engineer.

Decompressing Compressors
As you find yourself starting this section, you may not even know what a compressor is. By the time you finish this section, you may know what one is, but you may still not know how to use one effectively. That's because there is no other piece of audio gear that takes more hands-on experience to master than the compressor. This section could be likened unto a single lesson on how to play chess. Yes, you can learn the basics of the game and the movements of the pieces in one sitting, but it will take time and experience to become a master.

A compressor can be seen as an automatic volume control. It essentially limits the dynamic range of a signal. That is to say, that it will compress the loudest parts of a signal and compress it down so a signal is more uniform in its volume. The concept is simple enough, but the use of the tool will take practice. One reason for this is because the compressor is the one tool that is not working correctly if you can hear it and working correctly if you can't.

Let's look at what this means in practice. Let's take a look at our pastor's channel. Now let's say our preacher is a loud Apostolic preacher who speaks with incredibly loud peaks as well as very soft sections. Without compression, we'll have to continually turn the pastor's fader down during his loud sections and boosted up during the soft moments. Even the best engineer will be less than perfect in catching every nuance, and frankly, it would be quite tiresome after a short time. The answer to this situation is the use of a compressor.

The two most critical adjustments on a compressor are the threshold and the ratio. The threshold will set the point at which the unit begins to work. The ratio control sets the amount of compression that takes place when it does start to work. The ratio will typically range from 1 dB to infinity. Generally, soft compression ratios run from about 3 dB to around 8 dB. Hard compression ranges from about 10 to 20 dB.

Now, let's explain what these numbers mean practically. Your ratio is just that. If you are set at 3 to 1 on your ratio, for every 1 dB you go over your threshold, you will drop 3 dB of gain. If you go 2 dB over you drop 6 dB of gain, and so on. What does that sound like? Try running an iPod through your system and experiment with the two controls to hear what affect it has on the signal.

I will tend to start with a 10 to 1 ratio with most signals that need a good amount of compression and then adjust accordingly. What you *don't* want is to hear the unit working, or *pumping*. When a compressor is set right, you can visually see the reduction meter suck down on peaks, yet the signal remains at a constant level to the ear. Practice, practice, practice!

The more expensive a compressor gets, the more you will be presented with additional parameters to control like attack time, hold, release, gain, etc. These parameters simply give you more control of the compressor's characteristics, but your initial main focus should be on threshold and ratio.

Another useful feature you will find on many consoles is the ability to use another channel to trigger the compressor. This comes in handy when you wish to use a vocal mic to trigger a compressor on a playback channel to *duck* that channel down so the announcer may voice over the track playback.

It's good to remember that anytime you are compressing a signal, by its very nature, you are distorting the original signal. Therefore, use compression sparingly, but appropriately. It's a perfect example of where compromise is needed in sound reinforcement. Also note that the cheaper the unit, the more easily it will distort.

Equalizers
There are many types of equalizers available to you as an engineer: graphic, fixed, parametric, paragraphic, bandpass filters, the list goes on and on. Essentially, they all do the same thing. They adjust the tone of a signal by boosting or cutting frequencies. They will equalize the tonal spectrum of a channel by compensating for excessive or deficient frequencies.

The first thing to understand about equalizers is that all equalizers are not created equal. The quality of an EQ will determine how effective it is. A quality EQ will often get the job done by simply boosting or cutting a frequency by a single number or two while an inferior one may need three-quarters of a knob turn just to start to hear a difference. An inferior EQ will also tend to have much more overlap in adjacent frequencies in comparison to a superior product. Some equalizers are so cheap that they may even do more harm rather than good in some situations.

All equalizers will also have their own sound. Because an EQ distorts the original signal by nature, they will all color the sound in their own particular way. In the end, whatever EQ you're using, the general rule is less is more. The more you boost a frequency, the more coloration, noise, and distortion you will add to the original signal. Cutting is generally better than boosting as cutting will tend to reduce the noise floor as well as the frequency cut, but both boosting and cutting by their nature are still distorting the sound.

Anytime you are altering the tone of a sound with EQ, it's important to understand that the frequency that you're centered on is not the only tone you are affecting. On a typical one-third octave 31 band graphic EQ, you will boost or cut adjacent frequencies on the graph approximately half of the center frequency that you're touching. So if you cut 1K by 6 dB, you will be typically cutting 800 Hz and 1.2K by 3 dB at the same time without actually lowering the sliders. Constant Q equalizers will try to compensate for this effect, but with any EQ, there is still overlap.

Reverb

Most people know what reverberation is, but fewer understand how to effectively use it to enhance a mix. Reverb gives the engineer the opportunity to place an instrument or voice in any acoustic space for the purpose of enhancing it. We've come a long way from the early days of reverb simulation where springs and plates were used to simulate the effect.

Today's modern processors use actual algorithms that simulate real-world acoustics at the whim of the engineer, and with multiple units available built right into today's digital consoles, it's possible to have multiple instruments in completely different acoustic environments. Why is that important? Because a voice might sound great in one acoustical space, and a snare might sound great in a completely different one.

The first consideration when utilizing reverb is to ask yourself a simple question; are you mixing in an environment that needs any additional reverb? If you're in a particularly live room and you're having trouble getting intelligibility to begin with, you'll likely shoot your mix in the foot and make matters worse by adding more reverb to your problem. In these situations, use very little, or simply don't.

If you're blessed with a dead space or you're mixing outside, you'll have much more freedom to enhance your mix in creative ways with the added texture of reverb. The following are a few guidelines and tips, but generally, reverb is a creative choice. Your art might not look exactly like mine, but if you're new to this, try some of these methods.

I try to always limit the number of things in my mix that actually have reverb on them. In the 70s and 80s while everyone in the studios were going hog wild turning out records swimming in reverb, a band called Steely Dan produced a string of high fidelity records with very little reverb, and to this day, those records are standouts. I made a reputation for myself as a high fidelity engineer by following the same philosophy of less is more, spending more attention on using the effect to make something specific pop in a live mix, rather than covering everything.

With drums, I am only adding reverb to snare and toms. Cymbals, kick, and hat never get it as it tends to only clutter. If I'm in a very dead room I will use a very tight reverb with something around a 1-second decay, simply to add depth. As an effect, if I want to punch up a section, I might use a 1.6-second decay with a little bit of pre-delay in front of it, just enough to hear a short separation between the initial hit and the ensuing reverb. You can experiment with different songs.

Adding a little reverb to a drum machine or loop will do wonders when it comes to making it sound more realistic.

When it comes to EQ'ing reverb, try dumping out everything below about 120 Hz on the reverb returns. There's nothing down there that's going to add to the reverb effect, and having those frequencies in the mix will only add more mud to your mix.

The only instruments to which I might add reverb are strings and some horns. Get the reverb right on a sax or violin in the mix, and you'll be a sound superhero.

Vocals are probably the most likely place you're going to use reverb. Start with a 1.6-second decay and adjust to match your music and room. Remember that reverb fills in the space and time in between the notes. Long reverb settings do not work well with fast songs. Adjust accordingly.

Delays
There are a few guidelines when it comes to producing a delay that sounds musical in your mix. Remember, music is mathematical. Delays and echoes sound natural when they are on the beats, half beats, quarter beats, and double beats. Most digital delay lines will give you the ability to assign a tap button somewhere on your console. This is an easy method for finding the primary beat.

There are a few standard millisecond settings that will produce some classic sounds. 80-100 ms will produce a doubling effect, while 200-250 ms will produce the traditional *Elvis echo*. The difference between echo and delay is whether or not you're using repeats with the original delayed signal. A delay is a single repeat of a phrase, while an echo will repeat the phrase more than once.

Unless you're pulling out a good fifties doo-wop spiritual on a Sunday night, you're probably going to use echo sparingly. Delays can do more for you however, if you employ a few professional tricks in your mix. Try some of these. They will take practice to get right but when you do, you'll have a more professional sounding mix.

Do you have three background singers and wish you had six? Try running the background vocals into an 80-100 ms single delay and add just enough back into the mix to thicken the sound. When it starts to sound like an effect, back off, you've used too much. You'll know that you have the perfect amount when it sounds fuller, and you notice a big difference when you mute the delay. Do you want your three to sound like nine? Use a stereo delay with the left side at 80 ms and the right at 100.

Chorus

Grab yourself an old recording from the 80s. Don't those vocals sound great? What was the secret of that era? Well, it was the multi-track layering of vocals. A common technique of the day was to track a main vocal and then re-record two or more additional identical tracks to mix in just under the main vocal in the final mix. The result was a thick sounding vocal track. This worked in part because humans are imperfect. Try as you might, you could never lay down two completely identical tracks. Slight imperfections would cause phase differences in the additional tracks and thicken the original.

Today, we can electronically simulate this phenomenon by use of a chorus effect. The chorus will produce minute delays of the original material and purposely infuse them with phase differences and imperfections according to pre-programmed algorithms. The result is that thick 80s vocal sound....in a box.

Gates

Think of a noise gate as an automatic electronic switch. In its most basic form, you set a threshold to trigger the switch on or off. If a signal is below the set threshold, the switch, or gate, will not allow a signal to pass. If the sound raises above the threshold, the gate opens and sound goes through.

Gates work best when they are used on channels with a fast transient response like toms or a kick drum. They can also be employed as a form of single-ended noise reduction to auto-mute a channel when an instrument is not playing. The theory here is that if you have a channel with excessive hiss or hum or buzz on it, you can gate the channel off until someone actually starts playing the instrument. The sound of the instrument will then mask the noise, more or less. Obviously, this isn't the greatest solution to a noisy input, but it is an option.

The more knobs a gate will have, the more you will be able to tune the gate to meet your specific needs. One feature that might be added with these additional controls is the ability to adjust how far it turns the channel down, instead of simply turning it off. You might also have controls to adjust how fast it mutes down or comes back. All of these added controls are the manufacturers attempt to make the gate more suitable for a wider variety of situations.

Chapter 17

Monitor World

In the professional sound reinforcement industry, your monitor system is referred to as *monitor world*. That's because it's a separate world unto itself, separate from what's going on out at front of house. It has its own separate issues, methods, and problems, and it does so at the same time that the house is doing its own thing.

The purpose of the monitor mix is for the onstage musicians to monitor their own sound and the sound of the others onstage. This can be as simple as a mono mix that is shared by everyone or as complex as a stereo in-ear monitor mix for each individual.

Monitor Mix From the House

It's ironic to consider that the hardest way to do monitors is also the most common and that's *monitors from the house*. In this method, the sound engineer is not only mixing the service for the congregation, but he's also mixing one or more other separate mixes for the musicians on the stage. Other than perhaps listening every now and then in headphones, he is usually flying blind on the stage mix as he is not really able to hear them while mixing front of house.

To a large extent, church service monitors are usually *set it and forget it*. The sound engineer usually doesn't have to concern himself further until a change is needed onstage. For this reason, most church mixes are done from the house.

Monitor Mix From the Stage

As the demand for more accurate monitoring grows in complexity, a separate console and operator onstage may become necessary. Signs that one might be needed can be any combination of a frustrated house engineer who is having difficulty keeping up with monitors and house at the same time, to frustrated onstage musicians who have changing needs throughout a service.

A second onstage monitor engineer is not always needed with a separate monitor console. If a member of the worship team is capable of running a desk, often times you can get away with simply placing a monitor console on that person's side of the stage with faders facing the band. In this scenario, the churches sound engineer will set up and engineer the individual mixes initially, and then a worship team member takes over when a simple change is needed onstage, giving the musicians exacting control over what they are hearing, freeing the house engineer to concentrate fully on his world.

Tablet Mixing
With the advent of modern digital mixing consoles has come the ability to control the console from remote surfaces. Smartphones and tablets have given us the ability to step away from the console and walk anywhere in a church with the control surface in our hand. While this is a huge step forward in mixing our front of house sound, it really reaches its full potential with monitors.

Once a church has invested into a digital console with remote networking capability, it now has the option of adding the equivalent of an on-stage monitor console for the cost of a wifi computer router and an iPad. The software is usually a free download.

If the front of house engineer is running the monitors from his front of house console, he no longer has to guess what an onstage musician needs during a soundcheck. He can simply pick up his iPad and walk onto the stage with the worship team, stand alongside a member, and dial whatever is needed or wanted in the actual space. He has the added benefit of bringing his house console with him if needed as well.

With iPad in hand, the engineer now has mobile access to his house console, his monitor console, his house and monitor EQ and all of his routing and effects. When he walks back to his house console, the iPad becomes another touchscreen to be used to view any specific part of the house or monitor world to which he wishes to dedicate a screen. He might want continual access to the house EQ, the worship leaders monitor mix, an onboard digital recorder during the service, or any number of things. With some consoles you can even have multiple iPads running at once for multiple touchscreens. It's all about greater and more precise control.

Wedge Mixes

There are a few different ways for your signal to end up on stage. Monitor mixes can be heard through headphones, earbuds, in-ear systems, personal mixing systems like Aviom, or loudspeakers. Speakers can be anything in size from the humble hotspot mini speaker on a mic stand to a large floor wedge depending on the need. Though rare, I have even sent monitor mixes back to a stage as line level mixes to be plugged back into additional sub-mixers at musicians locations when an individual member had an onstage console of his own.

In-Ear Mixes

On the upside, in-ear mixes offer state of the art isolation and cure a multitude of problems. Because you are essentially plugging the monitor mix into your ears, you are taking the acoustic element out of the equation. Bleed issues, volume issues, all fade away. Because the distance from the audio source is essentially null, phase problems are also a thing of the past.

So what are the downsides or cons? In-ear monitors take more engineering than conventional wedges. In order for in-ears to work effectively, you must not isolate the performer from his acoustical space onstage or he will feel isolated and disorientated in his head. This does not lend itself to a confident musician. If you've ever tried to play an instrument or sing with earplugs in, you'll know exactly what I'm talking about. A vocalist will need to feel as if he's in the actual space he's standing in, even if he has his ear canals plugged with speakers.

The cure to the problem is to engineer sound into the performers head without losing the isolation and control that the in-ear system is providing. We typically do that by placing the room back into their head alongside the monitor mix. This is accomplished by stereo mic'ing the environment and placing those channels back into the performer's ears in a left/right configuration. Then the monitor mix is placed over the top of the environment mix.

To accomplish this, you will need two open channels on the console and two matched condenser microphones on stands. The mics are placed downstage left and right facing the audience. The same two mics are only there for ambiance reference so the same two mics can be used for everyone on stage who are on in-ears. Set the mic on the performers left into his left ear and the right into his right ear. Turn them up just enough until the room sound is natural in the ears of the performer. If you're too loud with these mics, they will compete and drown out the mix in their head, too soft and they won't be effective.

I have had national artists refuse to use in-ear monitors in the past. After talking with all of them, I found the cause of their apprehension was a universal problem. They had simply never worked with an engineer who understood how to engineer an in-ear system. After working with the artists, they all eventually were sold on in-ear monitors.

You should know that this system, even when done correctly, still has a learning curve for the musician. If you're used to hearing something one way for 15 years and switch to another way, even if the new way is far superior to the old, there will be a period of adaptation and adjustment. It will take time to get it right and to get used to the new method, so patience is the order of the day for both performer and engineer. This is normal.

Personal Mixers

Aviom and many similar companies are now making digital personal mixing systems for mixing personal monitors onstage. These little digital control surfaces typically get a sub-mix of 16 or more channels via a cat5 cable from the house console. These boxes give the individual musician the ability to custom tailor their own monitor mix into a set of headphones, earbuds, in-ear monitors, or wedge speakers.

The positive or pro, is the level of control each person has onstage. The con is the level of control each person has onstage. With control comes the responsibility of learning how to engineer monitors to sound good yourself, without the safety net of an engineer's knowledge.

What's in Your Monitor?

There are two main ways for a musician to communicate to an engineer that they have no idea what they're doing. The first is to look at the engineer and say, "You know, I have no real idea what I'm doing as it relates to sound." The other is to say, "Just give me a little of everything in my monitor." Both methods are just as effective. When, (not if) you hear those magic words, it's time to do a little educating with your musicians so they can get up to speed on effectively setting up a useable monitor mix.

A monitor mix is not a house mix. It serves an entirely different purpose and has entirely different resources available. You do not have thousands of watts available to you in a monitor mix like you do with the house.

This mix is a reference mix to allow the musician to monitor their world. The other instruments and vocals that are added to a mix are only the elements that are needed to reference their world. A worship leader might only need his vocal and acoustic guitar with a few other elements that may simply be needed for reference in his underlying mix.

* * *

A drummer may need his own kick reinforced along with the elements in his world that are needed to reference other elements on stage, like the vocals, and bass to help guide his playing.

A background vocal section may need their individual mic the loudest, followed by the lead, followed by any instrument that they would not be able to hear otherwise.

Each monitor mix will be a limited resource of acoustic power and as such, each person onstage should use critical discrimination as to what is actually needed for them to hear, allowing them to effectively do their respective job with comfort and clarity.

Monitor Levels
Every person on stage needs to realize that the monitor level effects the house level and the quality of sound. Many musicians are totally unaware of this reality. It's often your job as a sound engineer to explain this to the people onstage. After all, they can't tell from their vantage point unless it's communicated to them. The worship team and sound team are on the same team. The more you all work together here toward one common goal, the better your final outcome will be.

Monitor EQ
Monitor EQ differs from house EQ in the area of motivation. Typically we EQ channels in the house to adjust their tonality. Typically we EQ in the monitor system for control.

A house EQ will be set to make the overall mix balanced for instance, while an overall monitor mix EQ will be set to eliminate unwanted frequencies and knock down areas prone to feedback. Seldom will I walk up to a musicians monitor mix and feel like it would be a great send for an overall recording of the night's event.

It's not uncommon for me to drop out unneeded frequencies at the two ends of the audio spectrum in a mix. If I have a front vocal mix without any appreciable low frequency present in them, I may roll everything below the vocal range out of them compared to the drummers, or keyboardists wedge.

I'll also listen for any part of the EQ spectrum that's eating up my available amplifier headroom due to excessive frequencies. A monitor that sounds boxy in the 600 Hz region, for instance, may not only be sounding bad, but it may be eating up valuable headroom in the amplifier.

After the entire mix is EQ'ed and balanced out, I might use a 3rd octave EQ to pinpoint and reduce frequencies that might be ready to let go, given the chance. If you're trying to EQ a wedge to not feedback, try the hunt and destroy method of searching and identifying.

In this method, let's say that you have a frequency wanting to go off in the midrange. Narrow the spectrum in your mind to an area where you believe the frequency is centered. This area will get smaller, as you get better at identifying frequencies.

In our example, let's say we feel the ringing frequency is somewhere between 500 Hz and 8K. Start at 500 Hz on the graphic EQ for that mix and raise it 3 dB. It did nothing? Great, return it to zero and go through each slider until you cause the ring to let go. Bear in mind, once you think you've found the frequency, return it to zero and try the one above it. It may be that the first slider was only setting off the feedback because of artifacts and the frequency above it was the actual offender. In any event, one fader will give you the most response, and that's the problem frequency. Once the frequency is found, reduce it enough to eliminate the problem. If you get to a point where everything is going off, you simply know you're too loud.

Can I Have Some Reverb?
This is a common question that I get from the musicians on stage, particularly vocalists. Most modern digital consoles will have at least four built-in digital reverbs. Most services can get by on two

Chapter 18

Engineering Secrets Revealed

Now, are we ready to get down to it? This chapter contains the secrets and techniques that professional engineers use to set them above the pack. After you have basics mastered, learn these techniques to move to the front of the class, and engineer like a pro.

Mixing in the Sweet Spot
The single most important trick to high fidelity sound is the ability to know, understand, and mix in the sweet spot. Every part of the audio chain from the original source, to the human ear, has a workable dynamic range. Everything in that chain, including every piece of electronic equipment, has a saturation point. Even the room in which you are mixing will have a dynamic range of operation, and when the sound pressure in that space exceeds its ability, saturation is reached, and the sound will move from clean to colored.

Now there is a curious phenomenon that occurs with every piece of this chain. There is a sweet spot at every stage that occurs in the top 20% or so of the operating spectrum, just before the stage saturates. This zone is a sweet spot where everything sounds the best to the ear. If you can operate in that 20% everywhere, your mix will sound its best.

Frequency Dumping
Every time we turn something up on a fader, we are adding a multitude of things to our mix. The amateur soundman may only be thinking about a singer when he raises the singer's fader, but the experienced engineer is thinking about everything he's adding by raising it. Sound mixing is an accumulative process and as we add more and more elements to our mix, we also add more and more

or three just fine. With church applications, I will often take the last digital reverb in the onboard rack and dedicate it to the monitors. The reverb returns will come back on channels on your digital console that will have effect sends just like a normal input channel strip. Simply turn the return of one of these reverbs back into the monitor of the person who is requesting to hear more reverb. Now as a person asks for reverb in their monitor mix you have only to dial them into the reverb and it will return into their personal mix. Use a very generic reverb, 1.5 seconds of decay is usually just fine. If you find that this is too long and it's starting to clutter the mix, you can dial the reverb time back. Also, remember to dump out all of your low frequencies on that reverb from about 120 Hz down.

artifacts. Every time a fader comes up we add that element to the mix along with electronic noise, room noise, bleed from other instruments onstage, and so on.

The trick is to eliminate anything from a channel that is not needed to begin with. One way to accomplish this is through frequency dumping. This method can happen in a couple of ways, and typically a combination of two methods are used to get the job done. First, listen to your channel. Listen to the usable low end on the input. Roll off your hi-pass filter as much as you can until you audibly hear low frequency going away on the card and then back it down just a bit.

When I'm setting up a mix I am high passing just about everything but the kick channel and keys. Cymbals and high hat typically get the most cutting as the brass in the cymbals will bleed into all the tom mics. Harsh brass is hard to get out of your mix to begin with, so you're really just using these channels to add sizzle.

Before I even hear a vocal channel, I will have it high passed at around 120 Hz. A vocal channel or wireless headset will usually end up passed somewhere between 120 and 180 Hz. This is very important for keeping your mix clean as vocal mics love to pick up ambient room noise like HVAC systems, not to mention that they are almost always facing the band.

Isolation
The greater your isolation, the greater is your control. There are a few tricks of the trade you can employ when it comes to isolation. In small rooms, plexiglass cages can help to contain drums, but you can also do a lot to control guitars. Speaker cabinets for guitars and keyboards are quite directional and guitarists will tend to point those directional cabinets at the audience and at the back of their legs. If you have small guitar cabinets onstage, try locating them pointing up at the guitarist, slightly off to one side, similar to a wedge monitor. If your guitarist has a full-size cabinet, you might want to try a side stage approach, elevating the cabinet on a road

case or similar box to get it up close to ear height. The result will be a cabinet that is lower in overall volume, pointing away from you and your audience.

I once ran sound for a KISS tribute band that used expensive guitar cabinet simulator boxes on stage. These devices processed the sound like a speaker cabinet and output it as a simulated Marshall stack output at their stereo XLR connectors. They plugged into the PA system just like direct boxes. The result was a stage sound that was so clean, many people came up to me after the show and asked if they were listening to a recording of KISS instead of a live band. Only the drums and vocal mics were acoustically open mics on stage. Be forewarned, using a normal direct box for a guitar will not yield good results. You'll want an expensive guitar cabinet simulation device if you want to put this into practice.

Stereo Tricks
A good stereo mix will elevate your house mix to a new level. Not all church engineers have the luxury of mixing on a stereo sound system, but for those who do, use your stereo ability! Hard pans work in a few places, but generally, you'll want to avoid them as you will alienate half of your audience because only the people on the panned side will be able to hear it.

These are my stereo guidelines for coming up with an effective stereo mix. Toms are one of the very few places that I will hard pan and this is why. Generally, live drums bleed everywhere. If you pan overheads hard left and right you'll still have enough energy bleeding into all the other mics to effectively hear them from both sides.

When dealing with toms, our natural inclination is to pan them in the stereo spectrum as if you are the drummer and the toms are in front of you. Engineers will often pan three toms left, center, and right. Four toms at left, ten o'clock, two o'clock, and right. While this common practice will work fine, I have found that a superior method is to hard pan all the toms every other one. If you have two toms, left and right. Three toms, left, right, left. Four toms, left, right, left, right. This may sound odd at first, but let me explain why this trick works so well. First off, remember, drums bleed everywhere. So even if you're hard left and right, there will still be sufficient energy for every tom in your mix once the snare, kick, and overheads come into play.

Next, we'll likely be treating those toms with a stereo reverb that will further spread them out into both channels. What will happen is that the ear will simply pick up on the cue of the original stick crack coming from one side of the PA or the other. Even with hard panning, you will effectively end up with a 100%/70% mix of each tom in left and right.

But why not do the left, center, right thing? There's a good reason why I don't. Drummers seldom do a big roll from one side of the kit to the other. Instead, most tom hits are two adjacent toms. Boom, boom, and crash, or boom, boom and back to snare and hat. So effectively, you have set up for a great sounding stereo roll every time the drummer goes for his toms, even when he's only hitting two.

Next, everything that is available to take in stereo, set it up in stereo. If your guitarist plays through a stereo rig, put two mics on it and take it in stereo. Same for the keys, if the keyboard has stereo out, plug in two DIs and go stereo whenever and where ever possible.

Generally, there is no need to take a bass in stereo as the majority of the frequencies are too low in the hearing spectrum to warrant it. In my career, I've had two exceptions to that rule. The first is Micheal Bloodgood's rig from the band Bloodgood. Mike's rig took three channels on my console during the Detonation and Rock In A hard Place tours, a left, a right, and a sub. His head had a stereo processor built in and generated the stereo separation for me. The lows came off a line out from the head and went up the middle.

* * *

The second is when I run sound for Billy Sherwood from YES. The YES bass tone is a very high bass sound compared to a traditional tone and it has been a well-guarded secret in how to achieve it for over four decades. The YES bass sound actually eats between three and five channels on a sound console. I am but one of a handful of engineers on the planet who knows the secrets to the YES bass sound. Unfortunately, I cannot reveal this trade secret. As the saying goes, I could tell you, but then I'd have to kill you.

Main vocals will always go up the middle, but you can create a stereo spread with background vocals if you have a number of them to deal with in your mix. Slight panning is the secret here. Just enough off center to be able to discern a stereo spread. Once again, you're going for a left, right, left configuration. Just don't pan them too hard. You're looking for an eleven o'clock and one o'clock pan. You can further help create separation by throwing every other vocal out of phase.

Choirs are another place where I use hard pans. Again, the bleed is such that the voices will fill in the spaces in the middle and it will sound good in any location in the house. If I have four choir mics, I will throw them right, left, right, left. Did you notice that I didn't go left, right, left, right? Why would I do that? Wouldn't logic dictate that the left people in the choir should come out of the left side of the PA?

This is where the magic comes in and why this configuration works. If you're in the audience, you'll hear the direct sound of the singers on choir mic one coming from your left. You'll hear the amplified version coming from your right, stereo! The same effect is happening at the same time on the right side, in reverse. There is also the added benefit of greater gain before feedback when you take a loud open mic on the left side of the stage and send it all the way over to the right.

Mono Signals in Your Stereo Mix
You may be wondering, but what about mono sources? How

do we treat them in a stereo mix? There are at least three ways to deal with a mono source in your stereo spectrum.

Method 1: Pan the mono signal where you want it. You may have two mono electric guitars and want to place them in the mix so there is some separation between the two. You can simply and slightly pan each to opposite sides. In this method, you're being careful to pan just enough to tell that they are panned, but not so much that you're hearing a major imbalance if you're sitting on one side of the PA.

Method 2: Pan the mono source straight up the middle and add a stereo effect. This is in fact what you're doing with vocals every time you run them through a stereo reverb. You are in fact actually making them stereo. You can experiment on other sources as well. A thick stereo reverb can sound great on a sax or violin. A slight stereo chorus can sound great on an acoustic guitar. Experiment.

Method 3: Stereo mic it. This method uses two mics instead of one to produce an actual left and right signal. This method is popular for mic'ing overheads on drums, mic'ing pianos, harps, and with what we call XY techniques, even guitars.

With an XY technique, you're facing one mic diaphragm directly at your source, and placing another mic at a 90 degree right angle to it with both mic diaphragms touching, one just above the other. You can even buy actual stereo mics that have two elements inside of them in a forward facing XY pattern. These mics are a really great way to mic percussion.

Method 4: Create a stereo source. Wait a minute. Am I saying that you can take a literal mono source like an acoustic guitar and turn it into a literal stereo source like a keyboard? Yes, I am, and here's how.

Most modern consoles give you the ability to do two things not previously possible on most analog boards. The first is the ability to patch any input to any fader. The second is to delay a signal entering the channel. These two abilities are there for very specific reasons and have nothing to do with each other, however, if you combine those two capabilities, you will have the ability to create a stereo source, and this is how it's done.

Let's start off with a mono acoustic guitar plugged into channel one. The source doesn't matter, and it can come in by either mic or DI. The next order of business is to convert the single mono channel on the console into two mono channels. Go into the digital patching page for channel two on your board and set it to be fed by channel one. Now both fader one and two will be fed by whatever is patched into channel one. Next, throw those channels hard left and right. At this point, if you raise those faders, you'll still have a mono guitar in the PA as both signals are identical.

Now, wouldn't it be nice if we could add some space between those two sources? This is where the delay comes in because time and space are related. For every 1 ms of time you add into a signal path, you will effectively add 1 foot of distance to the ear. So, if you are able to delay the right channel by say 40 ms, you will have effectively added 40 feet of perceivable extra distance between your speakers. It's literally like taking one of the speakers and moving it forty feet further out.

The great thing about this method is that you can now take multiple instruments and place them in different locations in your virtual acoustical space. You might have an acoustic at forty feet and a saxophone at twenty. This effectively allows more instruments to stand out in a mix without cluttering each other because they are sitting in different acoustical spaces in time.

Be careful not to set the delay too short as it will run the risk of causing phase problems or too long as it will start to sound mechanical and robotic. The range you're looking for is around 10-80 ms depending on how far apart your PA speakers are to begin with. Experimentation is the order of the day here.

* * *

Stereo Bass? Really?
The above method will work with almost any source. I have had engineers pose the question, "What about the bass?" In most church circumstances you'll likely be dealing with a mono bass. Because of the low-frequency nature of the bass guitar, stereo separation is not a usual choice for church application settings, but there may be times when a stereo bass may be desired. You may work with a bass player that ventures out of the low rhythm tones and likes to climb the neck into lead instrument territory. If that be the case, there are ways to take a bass in stereo, but remember, you will have a difficult time discerning stereo separation on a bass instrument if it's not played in those higher registers.

A simple stereo field can be derived by throwing a mic and a DI left and right. There is a natural time separation of these two signals of just under 1 ms to the mic. You can increase the distance to the mic artificially without actually pulling the mic back by increasing the time. Set the mic channel delay to the desired distance by elongating its time by means of the channel strip delay. Remember, you'll be artificially moving the mic back approximately 1 foot for every 1 ms of added delay. Dial it to your desired separation, and then throw both channels straight up in the mix for a moment to make sure that you're not inducing any phase cancellation by your delay. If you can't hear any phase cancellation and you're happy with your great stereo sound, return your channels to a left and right position, and link the channels if you are able.

Getting a Great Recording
Contrary to popular belief, you don't need 24 tracks to get a great board recording. I do it all the time with 2 or 4. In fact, I've probably learned more about my mixing ability from listening to my own board recordings than anything else. Recordings don't lie. A stereo board recording will show you exactly what is going through your console.

Although a stereo board recording is a great tool for isolating your console mix for later study, it usually is not an accurate representation because not everything will be going through the console in a small venue application like a church. You might get a board recording home only to find out that it hardly has any guitar on it because not much of the guitar was going through the PA.

A great solution for this is a portable 4 track recorder. I personally carry a Zoom H4n digital recorder, although there are a number of competitors on the market. The Zoom allows for 2 balanced inputs but also gives you a pair of onboard stereo mics to capture the room sound. I will set the zoom up at front of house on a stand and capture the L/R off the console on channels 1/2. I will capture the room sound including the audience and instruments that are not in the PA as loud via the onboard mics on channels 3/4.

Now I will have the ability to mix the 4 channel down later via a computer mix-down software package like Audacity (which is free) or by using an advanced mastering program like Garage Band or Sound Forge. I'll add in enough of the live tracks for the recording to sound natural, usually raising those tracks at the end of the songs to capture the audience applause. Remember that you'll have to time align these tracks to the line in left and right because they are capturing sound at the console. Simply delay the left and right mix about 1 ms for every foot your mics on your recorder are sitting back from the PA speakers.

Voo Doo

The final *voo doo, that you do,* that will set you apart from other engineers, is to simply be good. Good engineering takes practice and experience. The engineer that I am at 60 is far better than the one I was at 20 or 40 for that matter. Continue to practice, practice, practice. Be observant and learn from others. Study recordings and live shows. Sound is an art, and artists continue to perfect their craft throughout their lifetime.

Chapter 19

Light Of The World

Today I sat in Starbucks waiting in line in my car for my Venti Pikes with extra cream and two sweet & lows. I looked at all the flowers and bright colors found in all of the planters in the drive-through area. While I sat in line I ran through the checklist in my mind of all of the things I needed to do for my lighting gig today. As I ran through my list and waited for my coffee it dawned on me just how much we take for granted with the colors and the diversity in the world around us. For a moment my mind switched from work to the beauty of what was around me. The reds, the oranges, and the whites in the flowers, the bright red wood chips by the drivethrough, even the brilliance of the early morning sky caught my attention. On this morning this junior lighting designer took a moment to sit back and appreciate the Master lighting designer.

The title of this book is of course taken directly from scripture. As sound people, we notice references to sound throughout scripture, but what about lighting? Are there scriptural references to lighting in the Bible? Actually, there are.

Like all sciences, time and time again, we see modern science catching up to what is recorded in the Bible thousands of years prior. These examples are recorded in scripture in plain sight for those who are paying attention. A simple example is when God tells us in scripture that he will separate us from our sin as far as the East is from the West. When we read that in our modern culture, we take for granted that it was not commonly known until relatively recent times that the earth is spherical, and not flat. The Holy Spirit specifically records that it is as far as the East is from the West, not north to south.

* * *

The concept of filtered luminosity is yet another great example that we can see in our modern age. Throughout the Bible, lighting elements are used as descriptive terms. Some of the most well-known references are in the book of Revelation where we see some of these descriptive terms used in describing Heaven. Some of the passages found in Revelation 21 are the most descriptive.

In Chapter 21 we read; **I saw a new heaven and a new earth. The first heaven and the first earth had disappeared, and so had the sea. Then I saw New Jerusalem, that holy city, coming down from God in heaven. It was like a bride dressed in her wedding gown and ready to meet her husband. The glory of God made the city bright. It was dazzling and crystal clear like a precious jasper stone. The wall was built of jasper, and the city was made of pure gold, clear as crystal. Each of the twelve foundations was a precious stone. The first was jasper, the second was sapphire, the third was agate, the fourth was emerald, the fifth was onyx, the sixth was carnelian, the seventh was chrysolite, the eighth was beryl, the ninth was topaz, the tenth was chrysoprase, the eleventh was jacinth, and the twelfth was amethyst. Each of the twelve gates was a solid pearl. The streets of the city were made of pure gold, clear as crystal. And the city did not need the sun or the moon. The glory of God was shining on it, and the Lamb was its light.**

It's interesting to note that all of the precious stones mentioned in chapter 21 are of different colors. Not only are the stones colorful, but they all appear to be translucent in nature. The equivalent that we can understand as lighting designers would be gels and filters.

Jasper, for instance, is a green, making the walls a brilliant glowing green, or in effect, an emerald city. The streets are made of gold, but scripture goes beyond that simple description to let us know that this gold is a pure gold. So pure in fact that it is translucent and passes light. The rest of the stones mentioned all have specific color temperature characteristics. Sapphire is a shade of blue while agate has circular patterns of brown on white. Onyx has different strips of color as well. Carnelian is deep-red in color and chrysolite is an olive-green. Jacinth is a deep orange and amethyst is deep purple.

As always, to read things like this in scripture and liken them to things in our realm is to think backward. Heaven, after all, is a dimensionality far more real than where we presently reside. As such, it is our gels and filters that are a poor comparison to what is real.

It's also fun to point out that in Heaven, the light source and power is Jesus. No other light source is needed. It will be His glory that powers the luminescence of everything.

Meanwhile on Planet Earth
Yes, this is a book on sound, and someday I may write a book on lighting. Being…. bi-techual, I wanted to include at least one chapter with some lighting basics as I see the importance of lighting in churches ignored quite frequently. While it is true that a blind man can hear the word of God and respond, never underestimate the importance and place that lighting has in our lives and consequently in our church service. Lighting points the way and focuses us on the things that are important. Even the Bible tells us that we are to be lights in the world. We are to be illumination and we are to point the way.

Church lighting runs the full spectrum from simple and basic to large-scale and complex. Over the years I have installed theatrical lighting systems in churches that ranged from six or so instruments to rigs that are larger than my entire production company's inventory.

Today, more than ever, lighting is an important and integral part of the church service, not only for directing the congregation's attention but for illuminating the stage for video and streaming. Proper lighting in a house of worship communicates a commitment to care and quality on the part of the church. It sets the stage for learning without distractions or shadows. Simple key lighting (front lighting) on the pastor will greatly extend the attention span of the congregation and help them focus in on the actual message.

It's not the size of a lighting rig that determines quality in the church setting. It is the appropriateness, choices of the fixtures and controller, and the competency of its operator. Prices have fallen on the various technologies today to such a point where there are good choices to be had for any size church with any appropriately sized budget.

Few techs today are equally at home behind a lighting console *and* a sound console, and there's a good reason for that. The worlds of sound and lighting are very different from each other. Both disciplines take a great deal of commitment to master. Because of these differences, there is ample opportunity for sound & light techs to annoy each other. Both sides will tend to view the other discipline with a bit of a superiority complex. For me, I'm equally at home behind either console, having spent decades learning each craft separately. For me, the war is effectively over.

So from my unique vantage point, I can share these truths with you. Each discipline is just as difficult to master. They share many of the same traits, such as the ability for a newcomer to jump in at a beginner level and begin to get results on day one. But, as with chess, you may be able to learn the general rules of the game and the basic movement of the pieces in a day, it will take a lifetime to master.

Because we're only taking one chapter to look at lighting, this will be a quick overview of the basics, a short primer with basic knowledge that you might find useful. We'll try to touch on a few points that you might not be familiar with and I'll try to anticipate a few of the common questions a reader might have.

DMX Protocol
Depending on your personal world, DMX is either a rapper

sentenced to prison for tax evasion or a digital protocol for controlling lighting. For our purposes, we'll obviously be focusing on DMX as a digital lighting protocol.

DMX512 stands for *Digital Multiplex*. It is the current standard method of transmitting data in lighting replacing the old standards of Multiplex and 0-10 volt analog. As such, it is not compatible with Multiplex or analog systems. In fact, plugging a DMX line into a multiplex line can cause severe damage to instruments and controllers, so be careful. Just because two pieces of gear have a three pin XLR on them, does not necessarily mean they are compatible. Always check to confirm that both pieces of gear are in fact DMX.

These days DMX can control just about anything. As the name implies DMX512 is capable of controlling 512 different channels of information. When more than 512 channels of information are needed, we simply add more separate lines of DMX512. Each separate line of DMX is commonly referred to as a universe. Most churches are totally capable of operating on one universe of DMX512. Larger churches and theatrical shows will commonly use multiple universes to get the job done.

DMX protocol sends out a string of information from a starting point to an ending point. Because of this, you cannot manually split a DMX signal. In other words, you cannot utilize a Y cable in the middle of a DMX daisy chain.

There are times when we do need to send DMX into different directions. For example, we may need to go overhead to a lighting truss, while another DMX line goes down to the stage for fixtures there. In this case, we employ a device known as an optical splitter. An opto splitter is actually the end of the first DMX chain and the beginning of all of the other splits that emanate from it, with all of the data streams being created optically isolated from the original.

DMX employs no type of error correction in its digital

transmission. Because of this, it can be susceptible to stray electromagnetic fields and radio wave interference. Always use cables specifically designed for DMX. A mic cable may successfully transmit the digital information from point A to point B, having the correct amount of wires inside the cable, but a microphone cable will not have the type of shielding necessary to protect it from stray fields. As such, mic cables will eventually lead to RF interference which will manifest itself in unpredictable behavior for your lighting rig. You may go months with a perfectly solid operating lighting rig using mic cables, and then one day an ambulance drives by and the driver keys up his radio and your entire rig blinks, or worse. More often than not, erratic behavior in lighting rigs can be traced back to the kinds of cables being used.

In some circumstances, interference may actually be caused by the data stream itself. Sometimes the signal may reach the end of the data stream and bounce back at itself causing interference. In this circumstance, we will commonly use a DMX terminator to prevent data from bouncing back into the line. A terminator is nothing more than an XLR plug in the last instrument in-line with resistors across the hot terminals to soak up the data before it can bounce back. If a DMX terminator is needed, they are easy to build with readily available parts you can find on the Internet. There are also many videos on YouTube that show how to build one of these simple plugs. Most modern lights and dimmers will have termination built into them, so terminators are not as common today as they were a few years ago. However, there will be circumstances where you might need them, and it's always a good idea to have at least one around.

3 vs. 5
In audio, we stick with three lines in our balanced connectors, and because of this, interconnectivity between gear is somewhat universal. This is not so with lighting. In lighting, we have two common pinout protocols for data, three pin and five.

Here's the difference in a nutshell, a DMX signal is a digital protocol that uses a two-wire signal path surrounded by a shield to drain off radio interference that might interrupt or corrupt the digital signal flow. In a 3 pin system, the data travels over pins two and three with pin one serving as the shield connection. In a 5 wire configuration, the same pinout applies, but two more pins are available for use as a second universe of DMX if needed. Because of this, 3 pin connectors are considered as semi-pro interconnects, and 5 pin remains the standard as the professional connector.

Because both cables carry the exact same digital protocol and information on the same first three pins, they can interconnect with 3 to 5 pin adaptors if necessary. Because the 5 pin method is the current professional standard in use today, I recommend staying with a 5 pin system whenever possible, but if you end up with a piece of 3 pin gear, know that you can still use it with your system, though it will be through an adaptor.

Conventional Fixtures

A conventional fixture refers to any lighting fixture that is not intelligent by nature. A conventional fixture is essentially a simple light which will be plugged into a dimmer channel for control. Dimmers will use DMX protocol to assign one control channel for each dimmer. The control channel is simple intensity. Therefore if you have a 12 channel dimmer and you set its DMX address to 1, DMX 1–12 in the 512 channel DMX stream will control dimmers 1-12. If you set the same dimmer pack to 2, it would be controlled by 2-13.

Intelligent Fixtures

An intelligent fixture is any fixture that has multiple channels and is capable of more functions than just intensity. An LED instrument might use 4 channels for functions like red, green, blue, and intensity. This fixture would use 4 channels of available DMX. Once we start considering advanced moving lights which can use 20 or more DMX channels, it becomes easy to see where we might begin to eat up multiple universes of 512.

* * *

Conventional Controllers

Conventional controllers are basic in design and are well suited for controlling simple one channel instruments like conventional lights via dimmer packs. They can control an intelligent light but your control will be severely limited and they generally lack the ability to do any complex programming or automation. These controllers are usually limited to anywhere from 6 to 24 channels with each channel controlling 1 data stream of DMX. You can, however, address any number of dimmers to a single handle on most conventional consoles. You might have 20 dimmers in a sanctuary running house lights and have those 20 dimmers assigned to one handle on your console for instance.

Intelligent Controllers

By contrast, intelligent controllers are designed from the ground up to be complex programming and automation tools. Although the basic function of these consoles is universal, their operation and programming are anything but. Every intelligent light controller brand has its own programming and operation workflow specific to it. Because of this, the operation of these boards will take effort to learn and practice in order to perfect. Seat time becomes an important element in determining just how proficient you will become on these specialized tools.

Additive Subtractive

At the start of the chapter, we began with the idea of filtered light and breaking light down into the various colors that we can perceive as humans. From a Heavenly minded perspective, I believe we will experience far more color in Heaven than we are limited to on Earth. I believe we are currently limited to a small spectrum of what is possible, and when we are transformed someday, we'll be aware of brilliance and lumination that we can only dream of now in the limited dimensionality in which we currently live.

In our world, we have two major methods of producing color, additive and subtractive. Subtractive filtering is one of the oldest methods. It involves using filters to filter the desired color that we want to bring out to the eye. I say bring out to the eye, because how we perceive color might be a little different than one might first suspect. Take a yellow gel for example. The gel actually filters out the color of the gel, passing the remainder of the spectrum of light that our eyes in turn perceive as the color that was actually filtered out. Strange concept to wrap your head around, right?

To further mess with your mind, the eye then takes in these filtered images optically inverted from its reality. The image actually hits the optic nerve inverted at the back of the eye and it's the brain's job to flip them back around. So in a sense, we see our world upside down and inside out. If evolution theory were true, early man would have had a hard time in the survival department with his inverted vision while waiting the thousands of years for evolution to sort out this stage of development. He would not have been one of the fittest, I'm afraid.

Gels take their name from the original material construction of the earliest filters which were made from gelatin. Today our filters are made from high tech plastics and are much more durable and reusable than *their* early ancestors.

While subtractive filtering happens on a CMY (cyan, magenta, yellow) basis, Additive happens on an RGB (red, green, blue) basis. Additive color mixing derives the rainbow of color by adding amounts of red, green, and blue together. This type of lighting can be seen with instruments that use light emitters instead of filters. An example would be LED fixtures which use light emitting diodes for the light source instead of a lamp that produces the full spectrum of light that is then filtered.

Safety Third
Whenever my guys are working in potentially dangerous situations at a venue, you will always hear us say to each other, "Safety third!" It may be a funny sounding jest, but it has a very sober intent, yet it is communicated in a comical way. Whenever a crew member hears this term, he is immediately reminded that our

intent for every show is safety first, *and first, and foremost.*

Lighting safety is every bit as critical as sound and in some ways, more so. In lighting, we are generally working with larger amounts of power with more critical power distribution. Almost everything we do in lighting is overhead. There is a sober responsibility on our part to make sure that anything and everything going on a bar overhead is safely tethered. Safety cables are cheap, and you should always have more than enough on hand to get your job done so that you are never tempted to hang anything without a safety line.

Coverage and Focus
No matter the source, whether it is a simple conventional fixture or a complex moving light, lighting really boils down to functionality and quality of coverage. You can spend thousands on instruments with impressive features but fail in your usage if you are not able to get good coverage and focus on your stage. Every lighting rig of every size always starts out with the simple task of adequately illuminating its subject. Only then is attention given to impressive aesthetics and creativity.

The Operator
The amount of lights that you have at your disposal in your system is never the most critical part. Once I designed a large rig for a one-off concert with a band at a church. The rig was large for the room and I had the ability to wow the audience with many tricks, lots of changes, and loads of candlepower. The highlight of the night came toward the end of the show, after a high energy, bright song. When the song was over, instead of the stage blacking out, I left a solid blue wash across the entire stage. Stage crew members pushed onto the stage a couch, a table, and a table lamp. The guitarist sat down on the couch with an acoustic guitar, reached over to the lamp, and as he touched it, I simultaneously killed the massive rig and lit the solitary 60-watt bulb in the lamp. The contrasting result was spectacular, and I did it with a common household 60 watt bulb.

* * *

Lighting shares an important element with sound. With both skills, the weakest link in the chain is the operator. I have seen marginal lighting designers get marginal results from massive arena concert lighting systems, and I've seen great LDs do incredible things with minimal rigs. If you are going to go into lighting, your number one priority is your own skill development. Only then will you be able to use whatever rig you have to its fullest potential.

Chapter 20

The Art Of Troubleshooting

The Art of Calm

The ability to effectively troubleshoot difficulties is usually needed the most about two minutes before the start of a service or event, or so it often seems. The art of troubleshooting is a necessary skill set that anyone who works in sound and lighting will need to possess. Have I mentioned we live in a fallen world? I know, you're probably sick of hearing that by now, but the fact of the matter is that sound is problematic. One of our key job descriptions as sound engineers is *problem solver*.

Here again is another major difference between the soundman and the audio engineer. The engineer understands his rig on a constructional and functional level. He thinks in terms of the audio path when something goes wrong. He pictures in his mind the path and when he hears something wrong, he can see in his mind where the problem lies.

As a problem solver, it's important to understand that you are the *keeper of calm*. What do I mean by that statement? On any typical Sunday, or during any rehearsal, the people on the team around you will naturally assume that you are the person in the room with your finger on the pulse of the technology and the wellness thereof. They will in a sense, look to you to know when it's *time to panic*. It is so important for the sound engineer to keep a calm demeanor and work a problem when it arrises. When the soundman panics, it sends a clear message out to all of his teammates that *it's now time to panic*.

We should be the solution to the problem rather than adding to it. Over my 40 plus years behind consoles, I've had generators quit during shows, mic lines go bad, boards die, speakers cook, main breakers trip, and a myriad of things go wrong at shows. Some things are so subtle that only I and perhaps the band and crew may know about. Other things are so obvious that everyone will notice and fix their gaze on you. You must react the same way in all of these circumstances. Panic has no place in the sound engineer's toolbox. The bigger the problem, the less time there is for panic. The great pilot is not the one who never gets shot down. He's the one who flies the flaming plane down to the ground in every moment of its descent, eventually saving himself and others through an incredible crash landing, and if he cannot save himself, so be it. The outcome doesn't change his heroic effort.

The Art of Trust

By the nature of your position, you will have a built in place of respect with the worship team onstage. You're not trying out for the position, you are in fact, the soundman. You have a built-in position of trust with them. It is important for you, and them, that you assume that position. If you're a set it and leave it kind of soundman, you'll lose their respect real quick, and if you think they aren't noticing, guess again. The soundman's position is generally an automatic place of trust until that trust is lost or forfeited. Then you'll have to go about the monumental task of gaining it back.

While sound checking, the team will demonstrate this trust in you by asking for your qualified opinion. They do this by asking things like, "How does this sound?" or, "Am I too loud?" They also trust your instinctual reactions when things go wrong. No one sees incompetence in you when things break down. They recognize that things do this in a broken world quite naturally and regularly. They watch and judge the severity of a situation by how you handle it, and they will judge your competence not on how quickly you solve a problem but by how focused you are in seeing it through to resolution.

The Art of the Detective

Let's take a quick look at a case study to drive home a point.

My company had installed a large-scale sound and light rig in a church. Both systems were state of the art and large scale compared to the majority of installs. The lighting rig contained a number of LED moving lights of various kinds as well as static LED fixtures. After the installation was complete and fully tested, it was time for what we refer to as *First Sunday*.

First Sunday, as the name implies, is the public debut of a new rig. It's always a fun day where the congregation gets to see the new technology for the first time. There is typically a lot of hand-holding involved on our part as we walk the churches techs through the basics of operation. It's also a shakedown time to see if anything wants to go south under real-world conditions.

On this particular First Sunday, a problem materialized in a moving light. This specific moving light was missing some of its functions and was generally behaving erratically, doing things like dousing itself as it was manually moved on the console. We tried all the usual things like re-booting the system and resetting the fixture after the service but to no avail.

I returned at a later date, ready to swap out the defective fixture if necessary. To my surprise, when I got back to the church, a number of different fixtures were now showing the same issues. Now, I'll buy one defective light on an install of this magnitude, but a number of them doing the same thing pointed to something else being amiss.

Upon researching the situation, I found a number of other LDs online had had similar issues with the same console, and we tracked it down to a mode that the lights had accidentally been put into. We corrected the problem and voila! The rig was once again working correctly!

I returned back to my city only to get a call in the following weeks that the original light in question was still having rotating gobo issues. As it turned out, we were not dealing with a solitary issue at all; we were dealing with two. The first major point that anyone dealing with troubleshooting needs to fully understand, whether you're a mechanic working on a car, an electrician wiring a house, or an engineer troubleshooting a sound or light rig, is that problems don't always come in neat singular packages. They are often numerous, and the more elements a problem has, the harder it will be to troubleshoot and the longer the process will take.

Tools of the Trade

As a sound engineer, it's safe to say that I actually expect things to break down or go wrong at shows. That is to say that literally every time I walk behind a console in a club, or an arena, or in a church, I am carrying tools. I am prepared for things to break down at every event, no matter how large or how small. I may go through twenty events in a row without a single piece of equipment failing, but I understand that like death and taxes, equipment failure is inevitable.

At large events my rolling tote bag of tools is common in my truck pack, making its way to every show that I do. For a church service, I will carry at the very least, a Gerber multi-tool in my gig box. If you have tools available to you at the church, know where they are, make sure they are accessible to you at all times, and make sure they contain the basic tools you might need to do a quick repair.

The Humble IPod

There are a few pieces of test gear that every engineer should carry. A few of these you probably already own and you're not even aware that they are indispensable tools of your trade. The first is the humble iPod, or smartphone with mp3 capability. Yes, iPods are for more than just simply listening to tunes. They are indispensable multi-tools that can help pinpoint a myriad of problems in a sound system.

The first accessory you'll need for your iPod is a simple mini stereo plug to XLR cable. These can be bought on many online sites, or they can be built if you're handy with a soldering iron. You might want two of these, a long one of approximately ten feet to use as a playback cable to connect your player to your console for pre-service music and a short one of approximately two feet to use as a test cable for troubleshooting components in your system.

With a short mini to XLR cable, you now have a handheld pre-amplified playback source that can be plugged anywhere into the line level patch points of a system to verify that a certain piece of gear is passing audio. Is a specific amp in a rack passing audio? Connecting the player to its input will instantly verify if the amp is working. Not getting audio to a powered wedge on stage? A quick check with your player will tell you if it's the wedges fault or the input wiring to it.

Another cool trick to use the audio player for is…..wait for it……an audio player! Let's not forget that we can actually put things on these players other than our favorite albums. An iPod can also hold test tones, pink noise, phase pulses, and any other audio that might be of help in setting up or troubleshooting equipment. Look online, there are readily available test CDs that you can load onto your player. Also, look in your app store for dB meter apps, signal generator apps and similar test apps.

One such app that I carry on my iPhone is a real-time analyzer app. Back in the day, I used a rack-mounted Gold Line RTA in my front of house rack. It was one of the most expensive pieces of outboard gear that I owned at the time. I would use it to pink noise and tune my PA. The modern app that I carry on my phone is accurate to within a small percent of that Gold Line, and I paid $9 for it. Not only can I analyze my main PA with it, but because it's mobile, I can take it with me onstage to aid in ringing out monitors and such. It also allows me to walk a venue with an RTA in my hand, taking readings from multiple locations, not just from front of house.

The Unassuming Battery
The sub one dollar nine volt or AA battery, or as I like to think

of it, the disposable one dollar direct replacement for the four hundred dollar polarity and speaker tester.

One day my wife and I were having dinner at a friend's house. They where in the process of listing their home for sale and they made mention that they believed that the home was originally wired for multi-channel home theater sound, but they could never figure out where all the wires went, or if it had indeed been wired in the first place.

Upon looking into the back of their wall unit, I noticed a large bundle of wires with stripped ends poking out of the wall. I asked the couple if they had three common household items: a Sharpie pen, a roll of masking tape, and a battery. They curiously looked at each other, opened a kitchen drawer, and handed me the items. I took the AAA battery and touched it across the leads of one of the wires. The left front speaker in the house thumped to life with a clunk clunk clunk as I touched the leads on the battery terminals. I popped a piece of tape on the leads and marked it *left*. Less than a minute later, the entire living room was verified and labeled. I smiled and handed the tools back to the couple who were staring in amazement and made some sort of MacGyver reference as they shook their heads.

If you can actually see the drivers you are testing, the battery will also serve well as a polarity checker. If you are comparing two subs for instance and you apply the positive lead of the battery to the positive lead of both speakers and the negative to the negative, both speakers should move outward. If one sucks back instead of pushing out, that box is wired out of phase!

The Art of the Signal Path
Whenever troubleshooting an issue, it's imperative to be able to think through the signal path in a logical start to finish manor. I commonly see people making the mistake of trying to solve an issue by starting in the middle or at random locations. Any time you have an issue in your system, the quickest and most efficient way of

pinpointing the problem is to start at a known point where everything works and go through each piece in a logical order until you find the part of the chain that does not.

Once you find the place in the chain where things break down, substitute known working elements to pinpoint exactly what piece is bad. Fortunately for us in audio, our systems have many duplicate pieces that can be used as substitutions. Think of the average sound system and think of how many common items duplicate throughout. Microphones, cables, speakers, monitors, almost everything in an audio system has duplicates that you can press into service while troubleshooting.

The Art of the Hand Grenade

There will be occasions where time is of the essence when it comes to troubleshooting. When you lose a lead vocal channel three minutes before the start of worship might not be the best time to systematically check every individual piece in the audio chain to pinpoint the culprit. In this case, the issue might be a bad mic, or a bad cable between the mic and a sub snake, a bad sub snake, or a bad snake channel. When time is of the essence, sometimes your best response is the hand grenade method. With this method, you simply grab everything you need to effectively replace everything that might be bad and toss everything suspect to the side to be sorted through and troubleshot at a later time.

Noisy Grounds

Hums and buzzes are the banes of sound reinforcement. These gremlins can be caused by many things. The move to digital consoles has greatly reduced the causes of these problems by keeping audio in the digital domain rather than analog. Gone are the issues of poor grounds in snakes that used to plague audio. Gone are many of the ground loop issues that could be caused by touching grounds between consoles via snakes. Today the most common causes of hums, buzzes and ground loops are found in the instruments and instrument amplifiers themselves.

* * *

Before we delve into ground noise, the first concept that we must understand when working with electricity is that electricity is always trying to find ground. Any electricity, from household current to lightning is always seeking the quickest path to ground. The next concept that you must understand is that your body is made of mostly water, and you will conduct electricity. If you place your body between electricity and ground, you will become that direct path, and that path can be fatal.

There are three main causes of ground noise. The first is noise making its way into the audio path through the ground itself. In this scenario, electromechanical noise caused by a motor or heating element finds its way into the audio path through the common ground or neutral of your audio system. The culprit might be as simple as a coffee pot or a fluorescent light with a faulty ballast. You can eliminate the cause by identifying the offending device and separating it from your AC source. In a pinch, you also might be able to isolate your audio path by inserting a transformer into it by means of a commercially available in-line audio transformer. Lifting the ground with a ground lift barrel may also break the noises audio path, but if the noise is in the actual AC line instead of the ground, only a transformer or removing the problem entirely will correct it.

The second way is caused by noise being filtered off to ground by way of two paths. In this scenario the noise loops between two devices as it seeks out ground between the two. This is what is commonly referred to as a ground loop. We can break the loop by lifting the loops path either in the audio ground itself or in the power's ground. In this scenario, we might use a ground lift adapter on the AC line of one of the two electrical devices thus breaking the loop. Be careful not to lift both the AC ground and the audio path to ground as you will now be left with an ungrounded and dangerous system

Which brings us to the third and most deadly of sources, the missing ground. In this scenario, stray voltage and noise are trying to get to ground but there is none available for whatever reason.

Perhaps there is a faulty cord or other malfunction. The voltage potential is looking for any way to get to ground, and if a person touches a piece of faulty gear with one hand and then touches a path to ground, the person will become the conductor and complete the circuit.

Years ago, I had a friend who was playing a gig. His guitar was plugged into his amplifier which in turn was plugged into a wall outlet. Unbeknownst to him, the PA system in the room was tied into a completely different electrical box, with a completely different path to ground. With one hand on his guitar, he grabbed his mic stand with the other. Stray voltage looking for ground, stopped its current path via the wall outlet and ran to the better ground from which the PA was operating. Unfortunately, his two arms became the conductors from one to the other with his heart being dead set in the middle. My friend was suddenly frozen to both systems as the electrical current flowed unimpeded through his body for what seemed to him like an eternity. He eventually fell off the stage, breaking the connection, and saving his life.

After forty years in the business, I have taken a few hits as well. Once I went to pick up a DI box at a show and the same scenario as above was in play. I happen to be holding the XLR cable that I was about to plug into it and unbeknownst to me, the bass player had plugged his bass rig into a wall outlet instead of our grounded stage AC boxes which we had supplied. As I reached for the box, a spark of electricity jumped between the metal DI and my gold wedding ring on my left hand. Fortunately, I was able to bounce back from the box, and with lesson learned, I never wore a wedding ring at a show from that day forward. Ground issues are often the culprit when it comes to noise in your system, but never forget they can also be a much more insidious and hidden danger. Check all your ground paths and be careful.

Chapter 21

Isn't That Special

Recently I found myself behind a console in a client's church, running sound for a funeral. This was a high profile service for a community leader and owner of a large corporation who was also one of our clients. This gentleman was well known in his community and church and his business was really the main business of the small town in which it was located, so consequently his memorial service was a huge community and industry event. Because of this, the church would be filled and a large tent was brought in to hold the masses that would be present to pay their respects and celebrate this man's life. My company brought in speaker systems for both an overflow area in the main church building itself, and we provided both audio and video for the large tent area so that the community could both see and hear the service.

Sooner or later as the church soundman, you will be called upon to provide engineering duties in some other capacity at the church apart from the normal Sunday service. It might be a funeral, a wedding, a special concert or speaking event. It might be at the church, outside the church, or at another location altogether, but eventually, you will find yourself working outside your comfort zone of conventionality. In these times your knowledge and experience will be tested as you will not have the safety net of repetition to fall back on.

Funerals
The biggest stressor of special events is that we usually only get one chance to get it right. With both weddings and funerals we are serving a family during a life event, and that adds a special kind of pressure to our job. While we strive to be kind and courteous every Sunday as we serve others, we will need to kick it up to the next

level for these special events. If it is indeed a memorial, never lose sight that you are serving a family during a time of great need. They will likely not be thinking as clearly during this time, nor will they be as prepared as someone would be if it were a wedding or conference.

One of your best resources during a memorial service is the order of service program. Most services will have a pamphlet that contains the songs, presentations, and basic overall plan of what will happen and when. Grab one and make as many notes as possible on it. It will serve as your guide and will take much of the guesswork out of the service. If you were to get ahold of one of my order of service handouts, you'd likely see every section marked with notes that might include what wireless mics will be in use for the segment or video cues noted. You would see any audio playback cues and the names of the individuals that would be talking or introducing.

Sound-checking and rehearsing is just as important at a memorial as at a concert or church service. Soundcheck as many of the individuals as you can before the public enters. This will not only let you hear ahead of time if you have a problematic individual who might be a shy public speaker, but it will also allow your speakers opportunity to hear themselves amplified through a sound system. Be patient, understanding, and informative with your speaking individuals remembering that they may not be accustomed to public speaking at all.

A common practice at memorials is the use of a public microphone for impromptu tributes and stories from the guests. By its nature, you will not have an opportunity to check everyone on this mic. You will inevitably have individuals using the mic that will not have a clue how, and consequently, the volume will be your struggle here. A trick that I will use in these situations is to turn the mic down a bit as each new individual approaches it. Very few people will back off of a mic that does not boom with volume as they start to say hello and give their name. If anything they will usually begin to speak up. Once they do, then you can inch the mic back up to a comfortable listening level for everyone.

Toasting Nuptials

Few services will have more joy than a wedding. At the same time, few will have as much stress. Almost every wedding will have a rehearsal the night before. Make sure you're present and take the opportunity to mic everyone up who will be mic'ed for the actual wedding. You typically won't be able to get a word for word tech rehearsal, but you will have an opportunity to get some basic EQ'ing done and you'll be giving the nervous participants opportunity to hear themselves on the system ahead of time so that it will be less of a distraction on the day of the event.

Talk to your musical guests before the rehearsal starts. It's a good idea to do a run through with them before the wedding cast rehearsal or afterward. Remember that your EQ settings will only be a starting point for the actual wedding because no one wears their suits and wedding gowns for the rehearsal. Try to sit in on at least one meeting with the bride, groom, and wedding planner to make sure everyone is on the same page and minimize the number of surprises that you might encounter at the rehearsal, or worse, at the wedding. Soundcheck every piece of audio or video that you might have during the service ahead of time. The night before the wedding is not when you want to find out that you have an issue with a track.

If you have a number of tracks to play back during a service consider using a computer-based playback program as opposed to something like iTunes. I personally use an app called SoundPlant, but there is a variety of them out there, many being relatively inexpensive. These programs are used by professionals at award shows, fashion shows, and sporting events to place tracks or sounds on individual keys of a dedicated computer keyboard for instantaneous playback cues. Once you use one, you'll never go back to relying on hit and miss music cues on an iPod or phone for critical events.

* * *

While we're on the subject of mission-critical cues, let's talk about the recording end of your life event as well. Most memorial services or weddings will need to be recorded for the family. I've heard horror stories over the years of the amateur soundman who forgets to hit the record button or pulls the USB drive out of the digital console before hitting the stop button. Life events usually only happen once, and you seldom get a second chance to get it right. Ask yourself how critical the recording is for that particular event. If it is indeed mission critical, use two methods of recording it so you always have a backup when, not if, disaster strikes.

You will have many things to remember at your event. A trick to help remember to start a recorder is to place a message to yourself on your console. It's not uncommon to see tape across the bridge of my soundboard in large bold print telling me to remember to start a recording!

* * *

Guest Speakers

You will become familiar with your pastor in a short amount of time. Running sound for the same individual every weekend will provide both of you with a familiarity in your sound workflow. But what happens when someone new steps up to the pulpit on a given Sunday?

Introduce yourself to your guest speaker as soon as possible and figure out what makes that individual relaxed. Does he prefer a headset mic? Is he used to a hand-held mic? Does he prefer a lapel mic? Did he bring his own wireless rig or does he prefer to use a podium mic? Remember that he's not your pastor, and he may have entirely different needs, and that's perfectly OK. Don't be afraid to adapt to his method if it helps with his comfort level. The flip side is not to be afraid to step in and offer an alternative if his preferred method is not working as well as another method might.

I have a long relationship as the front of house engineer with a progressive national act called *Circa*. Billy Sherwood of YES is the lead vocalist of that band. On the first show we did together, Billy was struggling with his vocal mic of choice, a Shure SM57. After noticing that he was having a hard time with it in his monitors, I muted his mic and walked up to him onstage. "Are you struggling with your mic in the monitors?" I asked. He said that he was. I simply smiled and asked him, "Do you trust me?" He laughed and said, "Completely," as we had already established a good working relationship during rehearsal. I then proceeded to unplug his mic and replaced it with a Shure SM58 that I had hidden in my back pocket. I told him, "Let's try this, if it doesn't improve, we'll just go back to your mic. Let me know." After another song with the 58 instead of the 57, he was happy, and we moved on. The important thing here is to be ready to offer solutions but to do it in ways that put your guest at ease.

Conferences and Camps

Your comfort level will slip away more when you have to go to an alternate location and run sound on someone else's system.

Whenever I'm in this situation I will always try to go in advance of the date to gather as much intel on what I will face at the upcoming event. If I'm able, the best method is to get into a car and take a trip to see firsthand what you'll be using. If that's not practical, do your advance over the phone, email, or Skype. Don't be afraid to ask a lot of questions and try to foresee anything that might become a possible issue.

Don't stop with the basics of the system itself. Look at the microphone compliment. Look at the equipment at front of house and look at the number and capabilities of the monitors. Make sure you bring anything with you that's not provided, and if you are used to a critical piece of gear, such as a particular recording device or particular mic, bring it. Talk with all of your people who will be onstage and make sure everyone is on the same page. You don't want your guitarist to show-up without his in-ear monitors because he had planned to simply go off wedges only to find out that the camp has none.

In some cases, you may find yourself with a breakout session in an area too small to actually need amplification. Don't assume that you're off the hook for the session. Your speaker might show up and say, "I still need this session recorded." In those circumstances, small handheld recorders are your friend. You may even be able to push a cell phone into service as a recorder, but I'd make sure that it's plugged into power, and the phone ability to receive a call or text is completely turned off.

Musical Guests

A musical guest can run the full range from a guest worship leader from another church to an international recording artist or a full on, touring band. Anytime you find yourself hosting a guest artist, make sure you do your advance work! Contact your artist as soon as you're able and find out the full extent of their technical requirements. Do this yourself. Do not rely on someone else to inform you of their needs.

* * *

If you're dealing with a local band, have them send you an input list and a drawing of their locations onstage. Neither of these items need be elaborate or computer perfect, but they do need to be accurate. Even with professional artists, last-minute changes do occur, so be ready to roll with the changes, and let your artist know that changes are fine but to please inform you as soon as possible so that you can adapt.

A professional artist will typically send you what is known as a technical rider. This may consist of a professional computer generated stage plot with detailed locations and an input list. These lists will often times list microphone preferences. A technical rider may also list needed backline (Instruments), and other requirements for the show. Don't panic if you don't have exactly what they're asking for at your disposal. Call their technical director or tour manager to advance what you *do* have, and find out if you will need to rent any additional gear for the event.

Chapter 22

Psycho Acoustics

Audio Engineer

I saw a cartoon once on facebook that had six panels. The cartoon was entitled *Audio Engineer*. The first panel was called *What society thinks I do*. It had a man standing in front of a huge complicated machine with a massive amount of dials and knobs. The second panel was titled *What my friends think I do*. It featured a guy installing insulation. The third panel was titled *What my clients think I do*. It showed a smiling waitress fetching two pots of coffee. The fourth panel was called *What my parents think I do,* and it showed a nice young man selling a little old lady a TV set. The fifth panel was titled *What I think I do,* and it showed a rock star on a stage. The last panel was called *What I'm actually doing.* It showed a psychologist talking with a patient who was reclining on a couch.

There's so much truth to that cartoon that it's almost not funny. I've chosen to close my book with the final skill that you will need in order to be a good engineer, the ability to understand and work with others. This is the skill of psychology.

On any given Sunday you can really take your job and divide it in half. Fifty percent of your job is that of the audio engineer. The other fifty percent is your people skills. Both are equally important and the attention that you dedicate to either should not be neglected. In fact, the only reason that the sound part is important in this equation is that it directly affects how we are serving the people. Regardless of whether you're a church sound engineer or an engineer at a national act rock show in an arena, the moment that you lose sight of the fact that you are there to serve your audience or your congregation, you will no longer be an effective engineer.

* * *

Whenever I am on tour with a band running sound night after night, I always have in my mind that I am actually working for three different entities. One-third of this equation is indeed myself. I am endeavoring to put out a product that I am proud of and can hang my name on, but that is just one-third of the equation.

The second piece of this equation is the artist. What I am doing behind the console is essential to the presentation. My goal is to reflect the final product that the artists or people on stage are trying to achieve. This is the essence of service.

The third part of the equation of who I am working for is the audience. All three of these elements must work in balance with each other if sound is to be effective. In a sense, the end result lies with the audience, so if you have to put a priority on all three, the audience would probably take it. Therefore my final decisions on things like volume in the room lastly resides in the audience's comfort. There have been times when I have mixed a show slightly louder, or slightly quieter then I would have mixed it if I were simply mixing it for myself.

Everybody Knows Two Things
My wife is also a lifelong lighting designer and audio engineer. She has had a saying throughout her career that I've found to ring true time and time again. *Everybody knows two things, their name and sound.*

It won't take long for you to understand the truth in this funny little statement of fact. Everyone has an opinion when it comes to sound. Sound is all around us. The average person will find it quite impossible to go through a day without the sense of sound. That familiarity breeds a sense of entitlement in us all. At the end of a service, almost everyone in your room will have an opinion about the quality of the sound that they experienced. Whether they are conscious of that fact and whether or not they are inclined to share their opinions is another matter, but an engineer is keenly aware of this truth.

* * *

If the sound is good, a person may sit through a service and never consciously pay attention to it. This in and of itself is a compliment. On a particularly good day, they might note the great sound to themselves, or they might even be inclined to share their opinion with you.

The opposite is certainly true. Engineering requires a bit of a tough skin. You will, no matter who you are or how good you are, have people voice their opinions to you in the back of the room. This is a fact of engineering life, and it is unavoidable. If you are easily offended or insecure in your ability to do sound you'll find these traits rising to the surface in your life rather quickly. In a sense, the first place that you need to apply your psychology skills, is on yourself.

Physician, Heal Thyself

Knowing that there will be an occasional sound and light helper approaching you is a fact of engineering life, so what is the best way to handle and respond to it? You will receive feedback from pew experts in many forms. It might be as simple as a scowl from a congregant who turns around and catches your forward gaze. It can be in the form of *Captain Obvious* who feels compelled to walk back to state the obvious to you when something goes wrong.

Whatever form it takes, you should think through the inevitable before it happens and decide on a game plan in advance for how you will respond. For me, I just look at it as simple data. If you think about it, as engineers we are continually processing data and making decisions based on the data at hand. As an engineer, I hear the complaint or comment and process it along with the correlating data that it might relate to.

For instance, I might process the same data in different ways according to varying factors. For example, the complaint might be a simple, "It's too loud." If the comment came from a person in the back two-thirds of the church, I would process the comment something like this. First off, I'd ask myself the simple question *is it too loud?* It just might be! So I'd turn it down. If it's not, I might ask myself *what* is too loud?

The same question might be coming from an elderly lady who is sitting directly in front of one of the PA speakers. As an engineer, I would recognize that the problem for her is likely a proximity issue. The point being that while the complaint in both of these situations was the same, the cause and solutions were different. What remained constant, was that the complaints were data to be addressed, not personal attacks to distract you.

The 10%

Know that whatever you do in life, there will always be the proverbial 10% that you will never please. You can pull off the perfect event or service, know in your heart that it was amazing, and still manage not to make everyone happy. People are funny opinionated creatures and there will always be a few that need to voice it on a regular basis. This is as true for the sound engineer as it is for the worship leader or the pastor himself. Where there is art to be found, so is the art critic.

Conclusions

As our time together draws to a close and we look back over all of the technical areas we've addressed, I'd like to leave you with a few thoughts.

First off, don't lose sight of the fact that sound reinforcement is a team sport. You can be an absolute wizard behind the console, but if there is enmity between you and the people on stage, it won't matter how great you are at your craft. People skills will be the most important skills that you will need to practice as a sound engineer.

While I've made a living out of providing sound and engineering duties for a who's who of the music industry, I've had the blessing in my life to work with a few outstanding artists whom I consider not just clients but *my* bands and *my* friends. There are those few artists where our relationship transcends that of business. It's a very short list, but it's a stellar one. On that short list, you'll find acts like Bloodgood, Barren Cross, Slim Man, and members of YES and Toto. While these relationships were originally forged out of a respect for our mutual talents, they remain strong through the years because we've strengthened our relationships and friendships over the years together.

Trust me when I tell you that there are actually bad engineers on the road doing sound night after night for national acts. They are there for no other reason than people simply like them on a personal level. They're easy to get along with, and they don't cause problems or contentions. The golden combination is to be that person that people like and can work with *and* a skilled high fidelity engineer. Now you've become irreplaceable.

Also, remember that while head knowledge is very helpful when it comes to sound, the most important thing is the ability to use that knowledge to properly influence your mixing decisions, and that is a skill that comes over a lifetime of practice. There is no substitute for seat time when it comes to sound engineering. Knowing a lot of sound science in your head will do nothing for you until you learn how those things are applied in the real world.

Lastly, there is a comical saying out there that goes something like this; "I've taught you everything you know, but I haven't taught you everything that *I know*." I'll leave you with that as well, not out of arrogance but as an inescapable fact. In the end, I can give you lots of head knowledge, but your life experiences will truly be the unique thing that sets you apart in your craft. The time that you choose to put into learning it and perfecting it will be the final determination of how effective you will be as a sound engineer.

There may be fast tracks to more knowledge, but there are no substitutions for hard work at a sound desk. I hope I have given you some new tools and encouragement to go out there and engineer. In the end, there is no magic wand to great sound. There are only the results we have when we combine the knowledge of what we've gained with the skills we've learned over time.

May God bless you in your efforts, and may you never stop learning. I'll also leave you with an exhortation that I instilled in my daughter. As she entered the professional entertainment industry in her own way as a Hollywood makeup artist, I challenged her to never see her craft as something that she has to attain too. It's great to set goals and continually improve at your craft, but you will wake up someday and find that life has gone by without you properly enjoying it if you focus squarely on what you think you need to be, instead of who you are at every moment. It's not about getting to a destination, it's about enjoying the experience of the ride. Stretch yourself, but enjoy the ride!

Lastly, again, remember the balance of that teeter totter. Have fun at what you do. Enjoy the camaraderie of working with your team. It's a gift. Enjoy the learning process as you go through life. But at the same time, remember the soberness of the fact that *faith comes by hearing*.

Other books by Paul Doty

Rubber Meets the Road:First Edition - 1994
Rubber Meets the Road:Second Edition - 2004
Rubber Meets the Road:Third Edition - 2018
Sex Positive - 2018
The 15 Minute Mac Book - 2020

Available on amazon.com

Find Paul Doty online at www.pauldotyauthor.com
Book Paul Doty for training and seminars at
authorpauldoty@gmail.com

Made in the USA
Columbia, SC
25 February 2022